BE TRANSFORMED

By the Spirit of the Living God

Contemporary Adult Bible Studies Focusing on Life's Real Issues

Perfect for Men or Women
Individual or Group Study

Written by Sharon Dutra

Be TRANSFORMED
By the Spirit of the Living God
by Sharon Dutra

Printed in the United States of America

ISBN 9781479188710

Dedicated to 'Sharon's Girls'

I used to think that 'girlfriends' were a misnomer. You couldn't be female, and be a true friend. But God has changed all of that. I have many wonderful women in my life now, and without your love, support, and encouragement, I wouldn't be in the place I am today. I thank you immensely.

I want to thank all of my 'girls' for putting up with me for so many years while I was learning how to teach you. I'm so grateful that you were patient with me while I became more skilled in writing this material in order to help you grow and change. You will always be one of my life's greatest passions.

And a special thanks to Teresa, my sister, who also just happens to be my best girlfriend. You have been my cheerleader from day one, and I'm so grateful to have you in my life.

****

Thank you to my church family, Oak Park Christian, for all the love you have shown me over the years. And to my pastors, Jim Shields and Mike Gunderson, for the

willingness to let my wings fly! And thank you to my immediate family.
I love you all very much.

****

Besides my wonderful Lord, there is one person on this planet who is the most important to me. I would like to thank my absolutely awesome husband, Michael, who has watched me grow from a fragile root into a strong tree. You have contributed more to my life than any other human being I have ever known.
I love you forever.

****

And to my God
The Father, Son, and Holy Spirit
I owe you my very life, and everything in it. I will never be able to repay You for saving me, both now and eternally. Thank you for the privilege of serving You.
I am overwhelmingly grateful.

CONTENTS

Foreword

About the author

Twenty two years ago, I was homeless, living on the street, and surviving only by a thread. I was so profoundly unhappy, that taking my own life seemed like the only thing that would ease the suffering in my soul. But God had other plans for me. From a life of addiction, homelessness, isolation, and self-hatred, Jesus Christ has transformed me entirely. He has given me strength, vision, power, and life. He truly restored *all* the years that the swarming locust had eaten in my life (Joel 2:25).

From my Pastor

The Word of God is "living and active" (Hebrews 4:12). The Gospel is the "power of God for salvation" (Romans 1:16). And we are made holy through the Word of God (John 17:17). Although the Holy Spirit working on us through the Word is all-sufficient, God still uses preachers to preach and teachers to teach. Such work on behalf of the Lord is a high and holy calling that is not to be entered into lightly (James 3:1). However, when the Lord calls and gifts someone to teach, he or she must respond. And has Sharon ever responded!

Since being rescued and redeemed by Jesus herself, Sharon has had an amazing ministry of teaching God's Word to women, particularly those struggling with life-controlling behaviors, abuse of all kinds, and levels of brokenness that only the Lord is able to truly repair. The studies in this book are born out of real life experience, both in the life of the writer and on the battlefield (spiritually speaking) of six years, through one small group discussion after another.

Sharon's ministry of the Word has proven effective. As I look out on our congregation on Sunday mornings I see one former addict who is now a children's Sunday school teacher. Another is now a university student completing her Bachelor's degree. I see still another, who now respects and loves her husband and children, and another who is completing rehab. And one who is loving her non-Christian husband to the Lord. I could go on and on.

May the Lord bless you and make you more holy through Sharon's written studies of His Word.

Mike Gunderson, Pastor Oak Park Christian Church

<u>Who is the best audience for this book?</u>

I want to first make it clear that you don't have to be a Christian to read this book. The very reason I started a 'topical' book (meaning a book by topics) was because everyone in life has some sort of issues they are dealing with. Many come from backgrounds of abuse and addiction. And some people have made it through life without many tragedies.

But we all deal with some sort of attitudes that affect our lives. It's not uncommon for most of us to deal with selfishness, envy, anxiety, fear of commitment, guilt, or forgiveness at some given point in our lives. So this book can be used by anyone.

However, it *is* Christ-based, because this is the foundation upon which I have built my life. Before I gave my life to Jesus, I had tried absolutely <u>everything</u> possible to dull my pain. I had tried so hard to 'get my life together' but I was miserably unsuccessful. But once I yielded my entire life to Him through an intimate relationship, my life began to change and blossom in ways I could have never dreamed.

This life is possible for **everyone.** Jesus died for the entire world, and He wants us **all** to experience His love, peace, joy, hope, and eternal life. It is ours for the asking, if we are willing to surrender our lives to Him.

About the book

This collection of Bible studies has been in the making for over six years. I began writing them to fill a need for my newly formed women's Bible study. We were such a different mix of women; on one end of the spectrum were women who were ex-addicts and had suffered abuse. At the other end of the spectrum, we had others in our gathering who were lifetime Christians. And some came to our group simply seeking the Truth.

I searched long and hard for Christian literature that would be able to help this diverse assembly. And I knew these women needed Jesus in a deep and genuine way. I wanted something that would really change their lives. I just couldn't find anything that was perfect for my special group. So I began to write my own studies.

Great for men, too!

My husband also leads a men's group. One night, he was rushed and had run out of material for his study. So he begrudgingly asked if he could use one of my studies for the night. It worked so well that he also started using them regularly in his Bible study group. Later, we also mailed a copy to our friend who was incarcerated, and he used them to help the other men learn more about Jesus. We weren't sure the material would work for the guys, but now we know they work for anyone who wants to deal with the issues in their lives that are keeping them from knowing and serving the Lord Jesus Christ in a more genuine and committed way.

How we facilitate our group studies

We begin every Bible study in prayer, as it is the most important part of the study. We start by asking God to forgive us of our sins, and to clear out anything in our minds that might hinder His Spirit from illuminating His truth to us. We ask for God to be our ultimate Teacher, and to lead, guide, and direct our class. After prayer, we then take turns around the table reading a paragraph of the text out loud. Anyone can ask a question at any time, and I often stop throughout the text to highlight or explain the material.

We use the New Living Translation Study Guide Bible, as this is the most easily understood Bible, that is still true to the original text. We also look up every scripture as it appears in the text and talk about how it relates to our lives. Many times, we will spend a few weeks on one study because we expound on the material by sharing our own insights, struggles, and victories.

Leaders or facilitators

If you are the leader of the group, it's a good idea to familiarize yourself with the material before you begin. You can either use the studies as a baseline for your own teaching, or you can act as a facilitator while the group works through the study.

Just to clarify, I often use just one line out of a scripture paragraph. This is intentional, and is not meant to take the idea out of the context in which it was written. But sometimes, the choice of the one verse perfectly drives home the point of which I am making. Of course, you and the group are free to read the text before and after the stated scripture I have chosen, as you feel led.

How to use this book

Be aware that there are often concepts in each of the studies that may seem a bit repetitious. This is intentional. Experience has taught me that most people learn best when they hear information repeated and rephrased frequently. There is also a common thread throughout the book that emphasizes our need for Jesus, the steps we need to achieve a close relationship with Him, and the resulting benefits that will enable us to live a victorious Christian life. You will often hear the words peace, joy, power, and hope!

There is a lot of thought-provoking material in these studies. It is best if you just take a few sections per setting, and really spend some time thinking and talking about them. If you just fly through it, you'll miss the deep truths that are written in them.

At the end of each chapter, there are some questions under the heading called "Reflection". There are no right or wrong answers, but most of the questions relate to something that was said in the text. Also, there is a blank paper provided on the next page so that you will have room to write down your thoughts.

I have also written the names of the books in the Bible out, instead of using semicolons. For example, I write Matthew 12:11 and Matthew 14:10, instead of Matthew 12:11; 14:10. This is also intentional. Some people have never read the Bible, and they don't yet know how to search for scriptures. I have also written in plain language so that everyone can understand it. But I've also put some more difficult words in, so people can increase their word vocabulary!

<u>A note for those who are reading this book individually.</u>

I have made the studies as easy to read and reference as possible, because you won't have the group setting in which to ask questions or share your knowledge. But as you work through the sections at your own pace, you will learn a lot about yourself.

- FYI: The 'dot' used throughout the studies is a sign to stop, contemplate, discuss, and/or write down your thoughts and feelings to the questions.

When I use the words "the world" in the studies, I am referring to people outside of the Christian faith. It also includes the 'world system', which embraces values, thoughts, and customs that are not scriptural.

I would very much appreciate you sharing this book with your pastor, or the leaders of the men's and women's small groups you have in your church.

Due to the years of work that it took to prepare these studies, I do not want this book reprinted or recopied in any way. Only if enough books are sold, will it lead to a 2nd book so that more studies are available to you and others. So please help me out by NOT making copies, but by purchasing the book. And you can tell your friends how to get their copies!

If you would like to purchase another book, or make any comments, Please visit me at my website:

betransformedministries.com.

Or by email: betransformed@betransformedministries.com

And finally, you can always reach me by snail mail:

Sharon Dutra

PO Box 597

Grover Beach, CA 93433

facebook.com/betransformedministries

Thank you for your interest in my work! I pray that the Lord will deepen your relationship with Himself, and you will be able to gain new strength and insight in your walk with Jesus. This will allow you to make wiser choices in your Christian life.

sharon ☺

ANXIETY

'Worry immobilizes us; concern motivates us to positive, productive, action'

Anxiety is defined as 'a painful or apprehensive uneasiness of mind, usually over an impending or anticipated ill'. It is also an 'apprehensive expectation'.

Anxiety, depression, loneliness, and psychiatric disorders are rampant in our society. Hospitals, jails and mental institutions are filled with people who live in fear. There are more prescription drugs for these ailments than at any other time in history. And for all the advancements we have made in technology, science, and medicine, we find ourselves more emotionally, mentally, and spiritually crippled than ever.

As we look around, we might think that we are living in the most anxiety-ridden time in history. But mankind has always had problems with fear, and the Bible is replete with scriptures of God encouraging His people not to be afraid. Those in the Bible were familiar with persecution, famine, war, and horrible suffering.

Our gracious Lord knew we would only be able to overcome our fears and anxieties with His help, so He addressed this emotion frequently in His Word. While it's true that we do live in a time that seems to be spinning out of control, God's Word is the same for all generations, for all time. He knew we would be living in the twenty-first century, and He is still saying the same thing: Do not fear.

If you are someone who lives in turmoil because of your fears, there is real hope for you. If you have felt discouraged about your inability to stop worrying or being anxious, there is a solution. The answer to all of your troubles is Jesus, because He is the only One who is perfectly able to care for you, and offer you real and lasting peace.

Where does our fear come from?

Before we start our lesson, let me preface it by saying that there are some individuals who live in fear because of a true psychosis. They very well may need counseling and medication. But for most people who experience fear and anxiety, the core problem often stems from the lack of a close, spiritual relationship with God. Even people who have been Christians for a while can lose their intimate connection with the Lord, and thereby experience great emotional distress. The truth is, if we experience fear or anxiety regularly, a big part of it is because we do not completely trust the Lord.

This certainly doesn't mean we're bad Christians. But it does mean that we might need to make some changes in our lives so that the following scriptures become real for us. Psalm 27:1-3 says that the Lord Himself is our fortress. That means the God of the Universe is surrounding me and guarding me! Psalm 34:4 says "I prayed to the Lord, and He answered me. He freed me from all my fears". And "The Lord is my helper, I will have no fear. What can mere people do to me?" (Hebrews 13:6) We see from these verses that the more we turn our lives over to God, the less we will experience debilitating fear.

Another common cause of our anxiety is our compulsion to focus on ourselves. This tendency is not easy to overcome, because we humans are naturally self-centered. Ask any two-year-old! They are not taught to say 'mine' – it just comes automatically. This is the sin nature we are born with (Galatians 5:24; Ephesians 2:3, and Colossians 3:5). And not only are we prone to selfishness, but our society encourages it! We are bombarded daily with messages like "Get what you can!"; "Look out for yourself – no one else will!", and "I'm number one!" We are often raised with this mindset in our homes, and millions of advertising dollars are spent by companies that cater to this nature in us.

But this self-centered attitude leads to insecurity, because we weren't created to depend on ourselves alone. God created us to seek Him *first* for our provision, so when we try to fulfill our needs without His help, we become restless and frustrated (Psalm 37:3-5 and Proverbs 3:5-6). Think about the last time you obsessed over an event in your life. Did you feel better after worrying so much? Did your anxiety change the outcome of your circumstance? Probably not. The truth is that when we focus only on ourselves, our problems, and things that haven't even happened yet, we become slaves to our fear. And in reality, most of what we worry about NEVER even comes to pass.

Don't blame **me**!

Most people don't realize that when they fail to take personal responsibility for their actions, it creates anxiety. At some level, we all know when we have done something wrong. Blaming others for our misdeeds just delays the consequences we know we deserve. It's the same concept as if someone committed a crime, but didn't get caught for it at the time. They feel guilty, and look over their shoulder constantly, wondering when they'll be found out. They probably won't feel complete rest until they confess their crime, or they get caught.

Interestingly, the 'blame game' started way back when Adam and Eve began by accusing each other, God and the devil for their sin (Genesis 3:1-13). Neither of them wanted to accept the consequences for the part they played in ruining their lives. We used to live in a society where parents, teachers, and neighbors were not only allowed to call each other out on their sin, but it was expected. And there was a healthy shame in communities that effectively restrained people's behavior.

But we have now come to a point where we cannot even suggest that someone is misbehaving, or we'll be labeled as 'narrow-minded', 'mean', or 'intolerant'. We have become a people that are afraid to stand up for righteousness. We are continually faced with those who convey the message: "Don't say anything to me that might make me feel guilty about the way I live. It's my life and I'll live it the way I want". But if we look closely, we will see that many of these individuals are desperately unhappy.

Still another problem exists that fuels our fears - we are a spoiled people. We try to entertain ourselves into happiness with money, sex, power, material gain, substance abuse, and more. We dread the thought of simplifying our lives or giving our things away, because we don't want to live without our creature comforts. We detest the thought of disciplining ourselves, denying our fleshly desires, or taking the necessary steps to cultivate a deep relationship with God. The sad part is that because of our self-centeredness and self-indulgence, we forfeit God's gifts of love, peace, joy, and hope.

God did not fashion us to sit idly by, consumed by our own passions. We were created to be in relationship with Him, and to be interdependent with others. When we live in an isolated condition where the most important person is always 'me', then we are not functioning the way we are supposed to (James 3:13-16). In fact, the only way to lasting peace is to give ourselves to God, and allow Him to do what He wants with our lives. Only as we take our minds off of ourselves and give our lives away to others, will we experience real satisfaction. And only a conscious and active decision to put God first in our lives will release us from the fears that are caused by living life *by* ourselves and *for* ourselves (Philippians 4:6-7).

- Stop here and list three ways the "me first" attitude has damaged our society
- Think of three ways that your own selfishness might have damaged your life

How do I overcome this awful feeling of anxiety?

Not everyone who has anxiety issues is a completely selfish person. But Jesus taught us that putting others first is what truly makes us fulfilled (Matthew 20:27). We were created to serve God and to bring others to Him. Serving others that are less fortunate than ourselves fulfills our God-given role (James 1:27). Caring for others takes our mind off of our circumstances, and it allows us to realize how blessed we really are. This is a great stress and worry reliever.

We often put great emphasis on things that have no eternal value, which creates more stress in our lives. The most joyful people I know are those that trust in the Lord for their provision, and go out of their way to serve others to fulfill God's purposes. Their focus is eternity! When we worry, we crowd God out of our lives because we are trying to take charge of things that only God is in control of. Concentrating our efforts to advance God's kingdom will greatly reduce our stress.

Jesus spoke about how important it is not to worry in Matthew 6:25-34. He knew that our anxious thoughts would tend to be a debilitating problem in our lives. Negative feelings and attitudes are joy-stealers and relationship stranglers. While we do need to be practical in this world, we are called to *think* upon things that are lovely, pure, and right (Philippians 4:8). The great news is that we have God's secret to overcoming our fears, which is to seek His kingdom *first*! He'll take care of the rest!

- One worry that many people have is that their needs won't be met. Ask yourself this: When was the last time you went hungry? Or had no bed to sleep in or a roof over your head? Think of 3 situations that you felt worried, but God provided for you.

- What does the Bible mean when it says to 'put the kingdom of God first'?
- What kind of practical things can you do to begin putting God's kingdom first in your life?

Are you hiding?

An often overlooked aspect of worry is that we may be using our worry to keep us from taking responsibility for the things God has called us to do. At times we can actually feel *comfortable* stressing out! Our family and friends know the signs well - when we start to feel like we 'can't cope'. We have unknowingly 'trained' them to come to our rescue. We know we'll be free from having to take responsibility for our problems, because others will take over for us. This is how we use our anxiety to 'hide'.

This behavior may sound ridiculous, but often, we choose our old familiar patterns of coping, instead of making the effort to change. We even stay in unhealthy relationships for this reason. However, when we continue to use these old patterns of relating, *we literally waste our lives*, because no one is ever helped when we act like this. God cannot fulfill His purposes in us when we are self-absorbed. And we will never experience the exciting life that God has for us if we don't throw off our old nature (Ephesians 4:20-24).

Many Christians say "I trust God completely, with all of my heart!" But only one devastating experience reveals their genuine level of trust. Often, hardships cause people to become totally deflated. They lose direction and hope in their lives. The truth is, if we continually allow situations to overwhelm us, then we are really not living God's way (James 1:5-8).

Obviously, we will never be problem-free. But even in our pain and chaos, we can demonstrate that God has power over our lives. Even in the midst of the social, political, and financial decay we see in our nation, we *can* receive love, joy, peace, patience, kindness, goodness, faithfulness, gentleness and self-control from the Lord. He promises it, and His Holy Spirit can certainly deliver it (Galatians 5:22-23).

Negative byproducts of anxiety

Anxiety:

Damages your health

Reduces productivity for God's kingdom

Negatively affects the way you treat others

And reduces your ability to trust in God

- Answer each question carefully:

  -Are you in a situation right now that is testing the depth of your faith?

  -Are you using God's tools to handle it, or are you trying to fight the battle in your own strength?

  -Are you experiencing the fruit of the Spirit, or are you afraid, tense, and uncertain?

  -Are you having health problems as a result of your fears and worries?

  -Are you able to focus on helping others?

  -Do you have relationship problems because of your fears?

There's hope!

Training our minds to stand on the truth of God is the road to freedom. You can print the following paragraph and put it in your car, on your mirror, and take it with you everywhere you go. If you want to decrease your anxiety, you MUST get God's truth and His perspective of your life in your mind!

Our God is a God of *impossibilities!* He made the heavens and the earth. HE is the ONLY ONE in the universe that is stable, changeless, dependable, and trustworthy! He keeps the universe entirely under control, and He has all eternity, including every single second of my life, in front of His eyes at all times. He is ABLE to protect me. He is WILLING to save me and direct my life! He came to live *inside* of me so I wouldn't be alone.

What part of my life do I think He can't handle??!!☺

So, what should we be doing if it's not controlling the world?

As we examine our values and priorities, we begin to shed light on our fears. Our values are what we put 'worth' to in our lives. One of our responsibilities as Christians is to purposefully fill our minds with God's thoughts and desires. We need to take *His* character as our pattern, filling our thoughts with **His** ways of thinking (Romans 12:2). We need to find *His* will for our lives through His Word, His Spirit, and His people. This is the only way our lives will be free of overwhelming anxiety.

It is amazing that we humans continue to put our trust in our own 'wisdom', and in this changing, temporal, and false world. But if we put value only on *ourselves* and what *we* can do, we will feel unsure, because we instinctively know that human beings are unreliable and unpredictable at some point. We need to realize that people and circumstances change daily. If we are building our lives on these fluctuating circumstances, Jesus says it's like building a house in the sand (Matthew 7:21-27)! Nothing in this world is secure and unchanging except God Himself. Focusing on the things that concern our Lord brings us mental, emotional, relational, and even physical stability.

As Christians, we are called to deal with our problems in a godly fashion, and to bring our flesh into obedience (Romans 8:13). And God *wants* us to depend on Him with our whole lives! Of course, trusting the Lord doesn't mean "Oh I've been thinking about Jesus so much, I forgot to pay my bills!" or "Jesus doesn't care about my bad attitude because He loves me no matter what!" We need to discipline ourselves so that we are taking steps to walk in God's direction. Jesus is not going to bless us if we sit in our spiritual lawn chairs our whole lives and expect Him to wait on us. But *as we cling to Him*, He **promises** to care for us.

Additionally, we need to beware of what we watch, read, and listen to. When we allow our thoughts to focus on fear-based newspapers and immoral media, we are filling our minds with downright LIES and deception. We live *in* this world, but we are not to be part *of* this world (John 15:19). It is essential that we focus our minds on the Word of God and get counsel from godly sources. We already know from experience that our ways and the world's methods just don't work!

We will only find the peace we are looking for when we 'fix' our thoughts on the Lord, and trust that He will take care of all of the unknowns and uncertainties in our lives (Isaiah 26:3-4). The more we strive to know Him, the better we will understand His character – and we will come to know beyond a shadow of a doubt that He is reliable. We will find that the more we focus on Him, the greater level of supernatural wisdom, discernment, and insight He will give us so that we can accomplish His desires. He will give us the power to die to our flesh, so we can live in obedience to His commands. This is the key to the Father's heart! His Holy Spirit will come alongside of us to help us solve our problems (Proverbs 3:5-6 and 20:24). As Christians, we'll find that nothing in this life will bring us more joy or satisfaction than when we are pleasing our Master! This is one great way to decrease our anxiety.

- When was the last time you prayed for an hour? Read the Bible for more than thirty minutes a day? Fasted? Wept for your sin, or for the lost condition of your family or friends?

  The answer to these questions will reveal how much we are focused on ourselves, which will directly correlate to our levels of anxiety.

Our values determine our focus in life

Since values reside in our hearts and minds, they are sometimes hard to define. But a simple way to determine our values is by looking at our actions. We know what we value just by observing:

1. What we spend our time *thinking* about
2. What we spend our money on
3. What do we spend our time *doing*
4. What we use our talents for

- Make a column for each of the values listed above. Then, write 4 things under each column that pertain to you. Be honest! This will help you clearly see your priorities in life.

Why the trials?

We all go through times of uncertainty. Sometimes we say, "I thought God loved me and promised to be there for me. So why am I going through such hardships?" We often question the wisdom of God, but the real problem is that we misunderstand God. We think that since He has the power to do whatever He wants, He should zap us out of our situation and make us happy! Quite the opposite, He never promised us that our life would be a bed of roses (Matthew 5:11-12; 10:16-39 and John 15:18-27). While we do have heaven planted in our hearts – the hope of a perfect existence - this won't happen while we still live in our physical bodies. In the meantime, God may use difficult circumstances in our lives because:

1. They affirm our dependence on God, keeping us humble. Just think, if we could handle life all on our own, why would we need a Savior?
2. Hard times can draw us closer to God (IF we let them)
3. Our trials (as we depend on Him), are a witness to others who are struggling through times of trouble.
4. Through our trials, we develop strength and compassion so we can help others when they go through difficult trials (2 Corinthians 1:3-4).

That is exactly where the unsaved and the Christian differ:

We have a God whom we can trust (Psalm 37:3-5)

We have a Shelter into whom we can run (Psalm 17:8; 18:1-2; 23:1-4; 61:4 and 144:2)

We have Someone whom we can expect to help us through every situation (Psalm 33:18-22 and Isaiah 41:10).

We know the One who can help us figure out all the answers to life (Isaiah 55:8-9)

God promises that He will give us the power to do all that He has called us to do (Philippians 2:13). If we are doing what HE has planned for us, which is focusing on Him and His priorities, then we will be in the 'eye of the storm' (1 Peter 4:19). Life may be rushing around us, but we will have security, direction, and peace. The best way to handle our trials is to become an active participant in God's kingdom. While we have breath, we need to focus on how to best use our talents, time, and money, all for the glory of Jesus.

- List two ways you can change the way you have been handling your situation. Think about how you can take steps to change your focus so that God becomes the center of your life.

Is sin the culprit?

This study wouldn't be complete without addressing our unrest because we are allowing sin in our lives. Sometimes Christians think "I can't be that bad - I'm not lying, stealing, or murdering anyone" – sort of what we consider 'the big sins'. But don't be deceived; the hidden sins may be the ones controlling your life. Quite possibly, we are 'addicted' to 'ourselves', letting our ungodly desires control our lives. Maybe God has cautioned you about the soap operas you are watching, the books you are reading, the movies or television you're watching, the addictions you have, or the people you are hanging out with.

If the habits in our lives are leading us to be attracted to someone other than our spouse, or makes us want what we don't have, or causes our affections to be turned away from God, then we are living in sin. Anything that becomes more important than God in our lives is called *idolatry*. Do you have a lust for money? Are you obsessed with your job, your kids, or other peoples' opinions? What about your attitudes – are you consumed with lust, pride, irritableness, jealousy, revenge, or gossip? These can start out innocently enough, but if they are allowed to continue, they *will* become big sins. And this allows the devil an opportunity to take you down; he sees your weaknesses, and he is ***always*** working to kill, maim, and destroy you (1 Peter 5:8).

- What or whom do you honestly put above God? Remember, it's what you spend your time, money, talent, and thought life on. Write down 3 things that come to mind.

<u>So, how do we change?</u>

Fixing our thoughts on the Lord takes the WORRY out of our future and the 'what-ifs'. We read in 1 Peter 5:7 that we are to cast our cares upon Him, for He cares about us. The 'cares' we read about in this scripture means 'to draw into different directions' or 'to distract'. This means that our minds are literally *fragmented* when we carry our own burden. We cannot successfully follow through on any God-given task when our minds are so divided. And don't forget that the enemy is just waiting for your anxiety to kick in so he can further torment you!

Putting God first is hard work! It takes practice, time, and consistency. We can start by training our minds to focus on *His* ability and *His* plans. When your anxious thoughts begin to overwhelm you, pick up your Bible, say a prayer, or recite a favorite scripture. This is not brainwashing or ignoring the situation – it is a renewing of your mind, so you can grow *through* your circumstances and understand the will of God for your life (Romans 12:2). You can only think of one thing at a time, so your anxious thoughts have to leave if you are focusing intently on the Lord. When we continually do this, our minds will change over time, because the Word of God is 'alive' – and able to supernaturally change us (Hebrews 4:12).

Another effective tool we can use to overcome our fears is to praise God. Two simple ways to do this is to read through the Psalms or listen to praise music. Worship is a really fun way to change our focus. It also helps to write down the ways He has provided for us in the past, because answered prayer always strengthens our faith. As you read the Bible, be still and let Him speak His Truth to you. He **will** reveal His power and will to us *if we are willing to listen and obey*. God alone is able to meet our physical, mental, emotional, and spiritual needs – every day and in every circumstance. When we experience His provision, we will learn to **believe** that His love, care, and concern for us is real and trustworthy, and that He will walk every step of the way with us. It takes perseverance and patience to overcome our old thoughts and behaviors. But freedom awaits us if we continue to choose the Lord's ways.

How do I begin putting God first?

We have already learned that some ways to overcome our fears are reading and obeying the Word, praying, praising God, spending time with other genuine Christians, and serving the lost and the Body of Christ. We understand that fretting is not going to help us grow. We know that stewing over other people's attitudes or problems will not bring us peace or satisfaction. Being anxious over world chaos does not change those events.

People are often concerned that when they are ready to change, they really don't know how to go about it in a practical way. Deciding to make God a priority in our lives doesn't happen overnight, and it's natural to wonder how we'll manage. It's obvious that we can't just stop what we're doing during the day and focus on the Lord every minute. We'll probably find ourselves in situations at work or school where we feel anxious, but we can't actually get into prayer or worship at that minute. Often, though, it only takes a minute to regroup our thoughts. We can always 'get away' to pray by shutting our eyes, taking a walk outside, or even going to the bathroom! We may need to do this several times throughout the day to get centered. Training our minds to connect with the Lord consistently is essential. Soon, it will become second nature, and the frequency and intensity of our anxiety will lessen.

Our choices really do determine the kind of person we develop into. And the foundation upon which we 'build' our lives will determine how stable our lives become. If we want the life that Jesus promises (John 10:10), then choosing to spend time with the Lord on purpose is essential. Many people say they have no time for Bible study and prayer. But if we put down the book we are reading, turn off the T.V. or stereo, or any other myriad activities that we've made more important than the time we spend with God, we *will* find the time. You won't get what you need just by saying grace over your breakfast in the morning, or with a quick thanks before you hit your tired head on the pillow at night.

Lastly, focusing on the Lord's plans and trusting in His provision does not release our responsibility for making wise, solid plans in our lives. Our relationship with God is a *mutual one*, so we can't quit trying or stop working (2 Thessalonians 3:11-13). But continuing to place our faith in God means that IF our plans fall through, or He has a different plan for our life, we know without a doubt that He will take us through it NO MATTER WHAT! His purpose is to empower us to live victoriously in this world so we can bring glory to Him and influence others for salvation. And then He will bring us home!

The time you begin to spend with God will bring you deep peace and joy. It will significantly reduce your anxiety. Having our thoughts centered on God and living out His purposes will even make you more pleasant to be around! It will save you untold misery now and throughout your life. Remember, what we fret about, and what we spend valuable and unnecessary time worrying about, oftentimes does not even happen! When we get to heaven, He is not going to care how clean we kept our house or if we wore the right clothes. He's going to look into our eyes and ask "Did you glorify Me? Did you influence others for my Son, Jesus Christ?" It's time to start focusing on God's ability to lead you into a victorious, fulfilling, and satisfying life. He will not disappoint you!

Planning is smart, worry is foolish.

REFLECTION

1. What are my triggers for anxiety?

2. How do I handle my anxiety?

3. Ask yourself: If I let go of my anxiety, am I afraid that part of my 'identity' or my personality will be lost?

4. What will I do with my time if I don't worry?

5. What is keeping me from choosing to refocus my mind from my anxiety, to God?

6. What are the benefits of holding onto my fears/stresses/anxieties?

7. What are the detriments?

8. What are some ways in the past that I have failed to solve my problems?

9. By reading this material, what are some practical things I have learned that I can do today to deal with my anxiety?

Prayerfully ask yourself if you are genuinely willing to be free from this part of your life that has become so habitual. If you fear letting go, tell the Lord. He can and will help you overcome your old nature, if you let Him.

NOTES

Reputation is what others think of you – Character is who you really are

ATTITUDE

If someone told you that you 'had an attitude', what would say? Would you be offended? Would you wonder what they meant? Would you try to justify the way you were acting?

This world is full of people whose attitudes are infected with hatred, selfishness, and pride. They continually blame others for their actions, and they defend themselves, even if they're wrong. We have become such a 'politically correct' society that we can't even confront someone's bad attitude without being attacked. And we are so hypersensitive that we cannot even hear constructive criticism without trying to defend our position.

We need to realize that our attitudes affect every single aspect of our lives, whether they are positive or negative. Our maturity level is shown by our ability to examine ourselves and then being able to allow God to change us so that we will become more like Jesus. So let's start by looking at what the word 'attitude' means.

An attitude is:

An opinion

A way of thinking

A viewpoint

A mindset

The way you feel

The way you behave

A position you take

An outlook

An approach to a situation

It's all about ME!

One of the major reasons our society is in such a mess today is because we tend to live in our own little world. So often, we get so focused on our own problems and pleasures that we don't even acknowledge anyone outside of our family. Looking at the definitions above, we see that our attitudes really do affect the actions we take and the choices we make. Our attitude also reflects our obedience, or disobedience to God in every situation we encounter.

While our attitude does encompass the way we 'behave', there is a deeper and more important aspect of our attitudes that stem from the condition of our hearts. The Bible says that our hearts are deceitfully wicked (Jeremiah 17:9) without God's intervention. A common problem that Christians face is that they get saved without ever examining the condition of their hearts and attitudes. In time, they start to wonder why they aren't receiving the 'abundant life' that Jesus talks about, and they may blame God or others for their unfulfilled life. However, the secret to living a victorious Christian life involves lining our lives up with *God's* will, not trying to make God conveniently fit into our plans. We can begin by asking ourselves, "Do I think that my attitudes please God"?

How do I know if I have a right attitude?

Jesus displayed the right attitude, and He lived out the perfect pattern for us to follow. But in order to live a righteous life, we desperately need the Holy Spirit's help. This is where we often fail – we try to live a 'good' life by using willpower and determination. But God's ways involve living a life of:

servanthood,

humility,

putting others first,

and dying to ourselves,

even as Christ died to Himself, for our salvation

Jesus died *on purpose* so that we could live in close relationship with Him. This means that *we* need to live our lives for *Him*, on purpose! He knew we would never survive the Christian life without His intervention. The truth is, God is much more concerned about our inner motives than He is with our behavior. He knows that if our hearts are right, our actions will follow suit. Remember, the heart is where our real allegiance lies. We may not realize it, but at the end of every decision, we end up doing what we REALLY want to do, no matter what we 'say'! For example, we may *say* we are Christians, but what do we *do* when we are called to help the poor? Or if we're surrounded by people who are insulting our Lord Jesus? Or if we are up against temptation? If we are really 'Christ's followers', then what do our actions reveal?

We may say "I love the Lord so much"; but if our selfishness keeps us from doing what God has called us to do, then our 'love' is only superficial babble talk (1 John 2:5-6). If we look down on others or ignore their needs, in essence, we are despising the Lord (Matthew 25:31-46). A hard heart and a proud attitude will ultimately affect our connection with others, and it will most certainly affect our relationship with God. We may find ourselves 'obeying' the Lord, without really *desiring* to please Him.

If we outwardly do what God asks, but we don't passionately love Him, then we are like a clanging symbol – full of noise, but missing God's intentions (1 Corinthians 13:1). We've all had our share of Christians who 'preach' the Bible, but they don't live it. We can often tell when they are 'obeying' the Lord without allowing Him to change their hearts (Matthew15:18-19). This kind of 'obedience' is called 'legalistic compliance'. They live a 'politically correct' form of Christianity, but it's easy to see they are lacking love, joy, peace, and grace. Doing the 'right thing' without the pure motive of pleasing Jesus is just as bad as not doing it at all. Throughout the Bible, God has grieved this attitude from His people. And this is the very thing that has driven many people away from the church.

- Let's discuss some of the ways your attitudes have impacted your actions this last week. List 5 things you could have done differently that would have better demonstrated your love for Christ.

<u>Does my attitude reveal love for the lost?</u>

It's not always evident, but on some level, all people know when they are living in sin. And somewhere deep inside, they know that God is the answer, because God has written it on their hearts (Romans 2:15). The tragedy is that sometimes when the unsaved finally do come to church, they are faced with a bunch of stuck up, selfish, hard-hearted people. If they see Christians hanging out in cliques, forgetting to say hello to new visitors, or looking down on those who are not like them, it leaves them feeling like they'll never fit in. And if the visitor is brave enough to return to church, they are faced with a long list of 'Christian rules' to follow. No wonder unbelievers equate their church experience with 'what God is like' and run for the hills! (Matthew15: 8-9).

Is your faith the kind that has transformed your life into being a servant for Christ? We know from the Bible that "Without faith, it is impossible to please God" (Hebrews11:6). So if we really have faith, then we believe everything that God says. We take His admonition seriously about reaching out to others, because real faith *always translates into helping others.* No exceptions (James 2:17)! A heart attitude of true love always displays positive actions to lift up the downtrodden. Are we weak, superficial 'Christians', just waiting for our turn to get to heaven? (2 Corinthians 9:6-15; Ephesians 2:10). Or are we the hands and feet of God, compassionately serving Him by serving others, wherever we go?

Can you imagine if *everyone* did *something* to help *someone?* If we just went out of our way once a day for someone else, this world would become more united. People would not feel so unloved and isolated. The world would spin on its axis if we all reached out to each other, thinking of other people as much as we selfishly think of ourselves. God saved us and gave us faith and new life, because He wants us to bring others into relationship with Him and fill them with His Spirit. Jesus died so that we could accomplish this. He sacrificed so that we would be able to overcome our selfishness and reach out to the lost. It is our **attitude** that determines whether or not we are successful.

If we call ourselves Christians, then we are responsible to treat others with love and respect. An easy way to examine our attitudes is by asking ourselves how we feel when a person comes into our church with torn clothes, smelling horrible, and cussing like a sailor. Are we the first person to offer him food or water? Do we ask them to sit next to us so they won't feel alone? Or how about the immoral co-worker that no one likes? Do you sit around gossiping about them, too? Or do you try to help them by inviting them to church or telling them about your relationship with Jesus? These situations reveal your ATTITUDE. We may *know* the scriptures, but if we are not *doing* them, we are in essence, doubting and displeasing God.

- Stop here and ask yourself how you treat new people at your church. Think about how you treat others who are not like yourself, or how you respond to those that repel you.

Remember, Jesus Himself dealt with the scum of the earth. That's exactly who He came to SAVE, for goodness sake!! (Luke 19:10). The people He spent time with were infested with sin - they were the 'unlovely' in society. But He loved them by *demonstrating* His love for them. They were fed and clothed, discipled, invited in, and *shown* the love of God. Jesus did not try to hide them away, ignore them, or pretend He didn't see them! He was not ashamed of them – NO! He loved them and saw their potential!

Think of it this way. What if Jesus had come to us in our sinful condition and said "Hi, my name is Jesus. I love you. But I'm going to stay as far away from you as I can, because you are so filthy. I love you, but I don't really have the time to visit with you! So long"! If He had treated us the way we deserved, we would have never received salvation! The truth is, that without Christ, we stink just as much as much as anyone who hasn't showered in weeks *just because of our sin*. No matter how 'tidy' our lives may seem, we are repulsive without the blood of Jesus covering us.

- As a group, write down some of the typical things you do in a week. Now ask yourself how many of your activities are done without pay, for someone outside of your home.

This is not meant to be guilt-inducing session. But it is meant to wake us up to the truly important things in life. Do you think God is going to ask you how clean you kept your house when you get to heaven? Or if you were super mom or dad by having your child in every school activity available? Or if you made enough money to keep everybody in the family 'happy'? Absolutely not! His primary question when you stand before Him will be: "Is anyone here in heaven because of you? How did you display My glory to your dying world? And how did you treat the oppressed, widowed, orphaned, imprisoned, and downtrodden?" (Matthew 25: 31-46).

<u>It's a mind thing</u>

One reason we fail to exhibit Christ to the world is that our minds are not under control. God's Word says that we need to bring every thought captive to the obedience of Jesus Christ (2 Corinthians 10:5). God wants our thoughts renewed so that we exhibit a life full of good works (Romans 12:2 and 2 Timothy 3:16-17). As we train ourselves to daily read His Word and then obey it, our minds will be *transformed*. Our desires will change, and we'll have an altogether new focus. We will begin to die to our selfish ways and instead, we'll *want* to give our time, talent, and money to God's purposes!

As we change, we can begin to loosen the 'control' we have on our lives (which really translates to running around busily taking care of *only* ourselves to meet *our* needs). When we truly trust the Lord to meet our needs, we will start looking around to those who really do need help. Jesus said that He will care for us *if we put Him first* (Matthew 6:25-34), so we don't need to spend an inordinate amount of effort looking out for ourselves.

Another problem with our attitudes is just plain old pride. Human tendency is to think more highly of ourselves than we ought (Romans 12:3). And we can deceive ourselves by thinking "I'm no drug addict, prostitute, thief, or murderer, so I must be a 'good person'. My life is running pretty smoothly in the 'Christian' department". But let's read 2 Timothy 3:2, and Romans 1:28-32. Some of the people linked in with those 'detestable' people are those that are critical, fearful, rebellious, complaining, and gossiping. Wow! When we are not under the Holy Spirit's control, we really are slaves to our ungodly, selfish attitudes, because we are slaves to whom we serve (Romans 6:16). If we serve our flesh (selfish, proud, lazy, critical), then we are not serving God, because we cannot serve two masters.

And one more attitude that robs us of the fruit and gifts that God has for us is negativity. When we choose to focus on the bad things in life, we lack the joy and peace that attracts others to Christ's work in us.

Negativity isn't new!

Sometimes, we wonder how our society has become so selfish, disrespectful and hopeless. But if we look back to the beginning of the Old Testament, we'll see that bad attitudes are not new to the human heart!

Let's read what happened to the Israelites when they were approaching the Promised Land. Turn to Numbers 14:1-12. Read the whole passage, and then compare it with the notes below. You will be amazed at how similar their attitudes were to ours!

We weep and cry (translated into whining and complaining!)	vs. 1
We find others to commiserate with	vs 2,4
We *choose* to believe our situation will never change	
We feel sorry for ourselves	vs 3
We *choose* to believe the worst will happen in our situation	

We try to run from our situation (possibly from God's very discipline or pruning) vs 4

We try to solve the problems ourselves

We attack those that are opposed to our negative attitudes vs 10

We attack those that are trying to help us by telling us God's truth

Consequences of our negative attitudes:

We miss out on God's best, and His blessings vs 12

We miss out on the very purpose He has determined for our lives

We forget ALL that God has *already* done for us (we become double-minded when we continually vacillate between worrying and praising God)

We waste our energy on things that usually will never come to pass, when we could be using that energy to make this world a better place

What we need to do INSTEAD of the above ☺

1) Fall on our faces (knees) before God and repent of our independence, our lack of faith, our lack of trust, and our stubborn, willful attitudes
2) *Choose* to BELIEVE that God's plan includes His best for us — Numbers 14:7
2) Fix our minds on what is true, lovely, and of good repute — Philippians 4:6-9
3) Determine to humble ourselves (i.e. quit rebelling) and train our minds on Jesus and His plan to get rid of our fear — Isaiah 26:3-4

Maybe you are unhappy, or feel like you are in a rut. You might think that your life is boring or you don't have a purpose. God's desire is for us to put off the 'old man' and become like His Son (Ephesians 4:21-24). Try going out of your way to help other people and most of those negative feelings will disappear!

- Stop here and write down 2 ways you can help someone outside of your family this week. Make sure it's a realistic goal. Helping others is a sure-fire way to remove your obsession with yourself. It will be sure to bring you more joy, satisfaction, and peace than you can imagine.

<u>What kind of an attitude do I have?</u>

We will know if we have the wrong attitudes if:

1) We are insensitive to others, doing what we want, no matter who is hurt by it
2) We are oversensitive and do nothing, constantly fearing that we will 'offend' someone
3) We are a 'yes' person, going along with everything (no matter if it is against our morals and values, just to fit in). This shows we think people's approval is more important than Gods'. People pleasers do not gain God's favor (Galatians 1:10).
4) We are staying in relationships that are influenced by negative people. (As an adult, the only relationship that requires your commitment is your marriage. You can do great good by being a positive influence on your unsaved spouse. However, if there is violence or cheating, there can be a biblical time for separation. Read God's Word for wisdom and seek godly counsel on this matter). But as far as friends (and most family) are concerned, you do not have to spend

time with them if they are influencing you away from your stand for Christ. It is very detrimental to spend large amounts of time with the ungodly or critical-minded people. Don't forget – you become who you hang out with! (Proverbs 13:20).

5) We are not taking action to get closer to the Lord by personal Bible study, prayer, and spending time with godly people
6) Our self-talk is degrading, and our communication with others is self-centered, negative, gossipy, or complaining

- What are some of the attitudes in your own life that you might need to change?

Okay. We've read all about our attitudes and why they are so important. We have explored some of our own attitudes. Now we need to know how to change our attitude so they're more in alignment with Jesus'.

What can I do to change my attitude?

The first place to start changing our heart condition is to repent. Ask God for forgiveness for the way you have been acting. Ask Him how you can become more of a servant. We need to choose to lay down our rebellious ways, pride, and selfishness every day. When we are sensitive to our faults, we can freely confess them and receive forgiveness, and in the process, we will become more like Jesus. We will continually become more righteous, because we are laying down our own desires and mindsets, and giving God the control. When our hearts and minds are transformed, we will be increasingly free to make wise decisions and live the way God wants us to live. We won't sin as much, and we will experience less turmoil in our lives.

Reading God's Word regularly will show us how to change. And God's Spirit supernaturally changes our attitude as we surrender to Him, so we can have the power to influence others for Christ. We can show others the glory of God through our smiles and actions. We can become an example to others, showing them how to work confidently through difficult circumstances, no matter how bad they are. What a great testimony to a lost world!

So let God come in and change your attitudes. Soften up! If you do not have a natural compassion for other people, ask God to help you cultivate this. He wants this for your life! Remember, the purpose for us being on this earth is to Praise Our Glorious God, and to bring others into relationship with Him. Other people are the ONLY thing that we will be able to take to heaven with us. Jesus' whole ministry on earth was centered around helping and healing OTHER PEOPLE. Are we to do any less?

The actions we take now are what we will be rewarded and crowned for when we see the Lord face to face (1 Corinthians 3:8 and Revelation 22:12). God adores you!! He *wants* to help you live a meaningful life of joy, purpose, and peace, with hope for your future. It all begins with a changed attitude!

REFLECTION

1. What is an attitude?

2. Why is my attitude so important?

3. List 3 attitudes you do not like about yourself

4. What are 3 ways God has outlined for my attitude to change?

5. What is a practical thing I can do next time my critical, complaining, or negative attitude arises? Will I commit to taking this action every time I hear myself voicing a negative attitude?

6. What is the main concept I have learned from this lesson?

NOTES

COMMITMENT

'Commitment' means to entrust or to devote something or someone to another's care. It also means 'to enjoin', or 'to deliver to for safe-keeping'. It's also 'a responsibility or obligation that takes time and energy'.

We see from the above description that commitments are made between two or more parties. We might make several commitments a day; to others, to ourselves, or to God. Commitments are usually made in a spirit of trust, as the result of having made a promise. As we commit ourselves to someone or something, we are implying that we will uphold our part of the bargain.

Unfortunately, we live in a world where we frequently see commitments broken. Politicians, businesses, fraudulent salespeople, dishonest ads, and swindlers abound! The list goes on when we think of the less 'important' broken promises that we experience with our family, friends, and acquaintances. They might tell us they will be there or do something for us – but we've all been let down before. We have also heard every excuse in the book as to why someone couldn't keep their word to us.

Maybe we grew up in a family where promises were easily made and broken. If this is the case, we can easily become cynical in our relationships. We probably have a hard time relying on others. We might have difficulty making commitments, or accepting them from others. We often have a hard time entrusting our time, our things, or our feelings to anyone else. We might even feel like we're not valuable to others, because we weren't important enough for others to take the time and energy to uphold their promises to us. And some people have a hard time believing *anyone.*

We may withhold our trust from others in an attempt to shield ourselves from further disappointment. While this gives the illusion of keeping ourselves 'safe', it really only robs us of our ability to have intimacy with others. In reality, if we completely stop trusting others, we end up losing the capacity to experience true joy and deep friendships, too. And when the mistrust we hold onto affects our relationship with God, our faith can be severely damaged.

- Stop here and discuss 2 ways your experiences growing up have affected your ability to keep your commitments today (positively or negatively).

How do commitments relate to my everyday life?

There are different kinds of commitments – some we make because we want something in return. Often, we 'barter' our time, chores, or childcare so we can have a reciprocal benefit. Some commitments are obligatory in nature, which means that we do them whether we really WANT to or not. Working, paying the bills, and doing housework are examples of this kind of commitment. We do them even if we don't feel like it, because the alternative has a negative consequence. And sometimes, we make a commitment out of sheer love – just wanting to please the other person because we care for them. By necessity, our lives are full of commitments; it is when we begin to dishonor our promises that we start to have problems.

There are various reasons for not keeping our promises (other than simply not caring). One reason we make, and then break, our commitments is because we have trouble saying 'no'. We commit to things because we want to please people, or we want them to think we can 'do it all'. We may feel we are weak if we can't do everything for everyone all the time. We might think we'll lose our 'popularity' with friends or family, and we might even become guilt-ridden if we cannot produce. But the truth is, it is much wiser to say no in the beginning, than to fail to follow through on your promise later.

Did you know:

That not following through on what you say you will do is a form of lying?

- List 1 instance where you failed to keep your promise lately. Then, write down one situation where you were let down when someone else failed to come through for you. How did each situation make you feel?

Why do I have trouble keeping my commitments?

Some people seem to effortlessly make commitments and keep them all! And there are others that rarely make good on their promises. Part of this may simply be a personality trait. There are those who can complete two days of work in one, and there are procrastinators. But this doesn't mean we get to just stay this way and give the old excuse "That's just the way I am"!

The biggest factor, however, that determines how well we keep our word is our *integrity.* My favorite description of this word is "What you do when no one else is looking". This is the essence of the way we see 'right and wrong' in our life. But our integrity is what our reputation is built on. That is why it is important not to just blurt out "Yes, I'll do it" when someone asks you to commit to something. WE need to count the cost of our promise before we decide to answer. It's much better to say "I'll get back to you", or "I just can't fit that into my schedule right now. Maybe next time". Then, we can truly make sure we are able to do what we say we'll do.

Developing our ability to say no because we have our priorities straight is extremely healthy for our spirits, minds, emotions, and bodies. Running around trying to please everyone is dissatisfying and annoying, for ourselves, and others. And spreading ourselves too thin rarely gets any job accomplished well. As we take time away from our responsibilities to rest and have alone time, we'll be much better equipped to handle our scheduled commitments. And while Jesus says that we are to give ourselves away to others, we are not to do so at the expense of our health, our families, or our private relationship with God.

Keeping my word

I think back to when I first got saved. One of the most important issues for me was keeping my word! I told myself "I'm going to follow through on what I say I will do – *no matter what*. My word is my bond! People will trust what I say, because they'll realize I tell the truth".

This may sound a bit ridiculous, but my old life was so full of broken promises and failed relationships. I couldn't be trusted to follow through on *anything*. When God turned my life around, I made sure I did what I said, even if it meant great inconvenience to me, because I wanted to be trusted *so badly*.

I have found it very satisfying to develop a reputation where others can trust my reliability. And today, I have no trouble letting people know that I cannot do something, because I've found that they appreciate the truth from me more than excuses or empty promises.

- What do you believe others think about your reputation? Do people see you as cheerfully dependable, grumpily half-heartedly helping, or a flake?

But I don't *feel like it!*

Another reason we might have a problem with commitment is because we are way more concerned about ourselves than others. Think about the last time you failed to finish a task you promised someone else you would do. Was it because you were too tired, too involved in your own life, or you didn't care enough about the other person's concerns to follow through? If this is the case, and we are honest with ourselves, we will admit that we are self-centered more than not.

Because our moods, feelings, and thoughts change radically on any given day, it is important to know that commitment is based on our will, not our feelings. If we frequently live out our fleshly desires such as laziness, thoughtlessness, or selfishness, then our character is weakened. This further reduces the resolve of our promises. But when our values are strongly placed the way God has designed them, then His Spirit instills the self-discipline we need to consistently make wise choices and stick to our word.

Granted, it certainly doesn't make it any easier that our world encourages compromise in our everyday interactions. There is lying, cheating, deceit, and dishonor everywhere. And whether we realize it or not, this mindset has some influence over us. We may start to think "My commitment doesn't really matter", or "Someone else will do it if I decide not to follow through." But this attitude is contrary to our life in Christ. We have the responsibility to tell the truth and stand by our decisions.

Remember, we are not supposed to run ourselves down helping others. Healthy choices involve taking care of ourselves. And making time for ourselves is *not* selfish. But if we are spending 95% of our time on our own pursuits, we are just being plain selfish. And if someone is counting on us to follow through, but we fail to do so just because we don't *feel* like it, this is simply <u>wrong</u>.

<u>No trouble saying 'no'</u>

On the other hand, there are people who refuse to commit to *anything*. These are people that have no problem saying 'no', because they just don't care. They don't want to be bothered helping others. Instead, they prefer staying in their own little world, doing their own little thing. But God has a real problem with this attitude. He even says that if we are not actively serving His kingdom, then we are *useless* to Him (John 15:1-17 and James 2:17, 20, and 26).

<u>Our commitment to God</u>

The most important commitment we will ever make is our commitment to God. When He is genuinely placed above everything else in our lives, He will supernaturally change the way we think, act, and feel, so that we become more like Jesus. He will also help us become people of our word. But it's only as we submit our thoughts, hearts, attitudes, and feelings to Him in intimate fellowship, that we will receive His power. It is our responsibility to stay close to Him. It's His job to change us.

We can lose our desire for this close relationship, however, when our commitment to Him is based on wrong motives. If we find ourselves:

Trying to *work* our way into His graces

think that He will love us more based on our performance

or are just trying to 'stay out of trouble' – you know "God help me out of this situation and I'll never do it again" kind of attitude

then we will lose our ability and desire to truly serve Him.

When these motives drive us, the focus of the commitment is really on *us*, not our love for God or others. Our intentions need to be purified by the Holy Spirit, because when our deep *desire* is to serve the Lord out of love, then our promises to Him will be full of power. We all know that Love is the greatest motivator in the world.

- Do you feel that the more you do for God's kingdom, the more He loves you?
- Read Romans 3:21-28 and Romans 5:8-9. Stop here as a group and discuss the fact that it was *God* who initiated our relationship with Him and there's not one thing we can do to make Him love us more than He already does.

Consequences of our failed commitments

Two common things that we as human beings do when we are trying to deal with our failures are:

1. We ignore the situation because we don't want to face the consequences, others, or ourselves, and
2. We let guilt creep in so we are immobilized.

Most of us have found that neither of these responses are healthy, nor do they help our situation.

It gets worse.....

We have already read that a major consequence of repeatedly going back on our word is that people stop trusting us. But things may get progressively worse from there:

After we have ruined our reputation, we may start to distance ourselves from others, because we realize how hard it will be to regain their trust.

We may feel ashamed of our behavior, which can affect our self-esteem

We might become so discouraged that we stop trying to remain friends altogether (or we may leave a job or a church) and just give up.

This kind of deep discouragement happens because our natural tendency is to hide from God and others when we continue to choose to sin. The longer we live in our sin, the less we have concern for other people. And we ultimately cut ourselves off from the wisdom and the love of the Lord (Exodus 6:9). The word 'slavery' in this scripture, as in most Old Testament verses, reminds me of our own slavery to sin. If we continue along this path, we will eventually stop listening to anyone who tries to help us out of our old life. This may seem melodramatic, but I have witnessed this behavior and its consequences time and time again.

<u>So, how do we improve the likelihood of keeping our commitments?</u>

Remember, when someone asks us to do something, we need to stop and count the cost of the commitment *before* we make it. 'Counting the cost' means asking ourselves:

1. Do I have the time and energy to follow through on this task?
2. Do I have the skills and talent to accomplish it?
3. Will it be on the top of my priority list when the time comes to fulfill it?

If you cannot answer yes to all three of these questions, then tell the other person you cannot commit to them. They may seem put out at first, but better for them to be slightly disappointed beforehand, than to have them find out you really couldn't do it anyway.

One positive motivator for maintaining our promises is having and keeping a good reputation (Proverbs 22:1). This might sound a bit superficial, but think about it like a bank account. The more we invest (in commitments made and kept), the 'richer' our reputation becomes. This is important, because the more others learn to trust our word and our character, the more God will be able to use us to minster to them in more serious situations.

In addition, the Bible teaches us that our reliable commitments form a solid foundation to build our lives upon. Character is built by imitating the Lord. Every time we see our promises through, the stronger we are for the next task. And as we continue to keep our commitments, this will strengthen our resolve to **stay** the course, even when others break their promises to us. And the best part is, that keeping our pledge is a way to honor God, and offer thanks to Him for what He has done for us (Psalm 116:12-14).

Jesus: Commitment Personified

God's blueprint for commitment-keeping was demonstrated through Jesus, who made the ultimate commitment in history (John 10:11-18). Our Savior could have just stayed in heaven, given us the Bible, and sent His Holy Spirit to help us. But He knew that we needed to see *commitment in action*. That is why He **voluntarily** laid down His life for us. Because He followed through on what He said He was going to do, we can now spend our lives with Him, both now and forever! And He wants us to follow His example by spending *our* lives for Him (Titus 2:14).

What would have happened if Jesus decided not to go to the cross at the last minute? What if He had said "I'm just too tired. Even though I promised to do this, it's going to be too much trouble. And people probably won't care if I do it or not. Besides, why should I suffer for those who will continue to just hate me anyway?" Wow! If He had turned away from His commitment to us, the entire course of the world would have changed.

But because of His tremendous promise, we have salvation today and eternal life after we die. Jesus also tells us that He will be there for us no matter what we go through. And He assures us strength and protection for whatever He calls us to do.

But my promise isn't *that* important!

We might fall into the trap of thinking that our commitments aren't nearly as serious as the one Jesus made to us, so, we feel we don't really need to keep them. We are forever trying to minimize our faults, and we make tons of excuses so we won't have to feel the sting of our negative choices and actions. But the bottom line is this: when we become Christ's disciples, our lives are to reflect His character and His values. The Bible says that Jesus' followers must be where their Master is (John 12:26). This means we are sitting at His feet, learning, imitating, and becoming all that He wants us to be. Being true to our word is extremely important to God, because He IS Truth.

- Say someone is asking you to help them move on Saturday. In one scenario, write (or discuss) what you would say if you are able to help them (remember to look at the three questions listed above that we need to ask ourselves before making a commitment). Then, write what you would say in a situation where you cannot help them. It may feel strange to do this, but practicing how we will respond in the future helps our minds deal with the situation when it arises.

What if I feel I've been let down by God?

We often try to justify our actions by blaming others, or by playing the 'victim'. One trap people get into is 'praying' for a situation, but their prayers aren't answered in the way they wanted. Instead of letting God be God, and answer them in the way He sees fit, they whine and complain. Or, maybe they have gone through a hardship and they blame God for abandoning them. They use this as an excuse to do what they want, because they falsely believe that God didn't hold up His part of the bargain. They blame Him for not listening, or not being dependable.

But this is irresponsible nonsense, and it's just a way to get our own way. If we are truly in intimate relationship with the Lord, we will understand that *we* are the ones to ask for help. We are the ones who wait upon our Leader. We are the ones to submit our wills to His. And we'll know that we are supposed to be in prayer for everything, but leave the results and outcome to God.

Just because we don't get what we think we want, we need to understand and trust that God is absolutely committed to us, and He will provide exactly what we need, when we need it. We are still obligated to live up to His standards, no matter how He may answer us. Besides, many times, what we receive from our prayers is comfort, strength, peace, joy, and hope. This often turns out to be much more satisfying than many of the things we ask for. And we can thank Him that He *doesn't* always answer our prayers the way we want! ☺

It is also essential to *believe* that Jesus is the only One we can completely entrust our lives to. Sometimes we will find that trusting Him is like walking through the fog at the beach. Although we know the ocean is there, we can't see it through the mist. But it doesn't change our knowledge or belief that it is there. Likewise, we may not *see* God working in our lives, but if we have faith, then we will have a deep impression that He is there, benefitting us somehow. And He has already given us every evidence that He loves us, through Jesus' sacrifice, and through His creation (Romans 1:20). Oftentimes, we just need to be still and *trust in His character.*

How do my commitments affect the Lord?

In reality, it is not God who lets us down, but the other way around. It might help us to realize how our lack of commitment affects Him! In Leviticus 26:9-12, we read about the awesome covenant, or promise, that God made with His beloved people, Israel. In fact, the entire Old Testament is written to illustrate the on-and-off relationship the Jews had with their God. We read of a particular time in scripture when God is brokenhearted, because His 'bride' is CHEATING on Him (Jeremiah 2:1-13). The 'bride' in the Bible refers to God's people. In the Old Testament, it was Israel, and today, it's Christians. As a matter of fact, one of the reasons Christ came was to bridge the chasm between the two groups (Romans 11:25-31).

When God created us, he knew that in our fallen state, we would never be able to completely hold up our part of this covenant agreement. However, we see God continuing to keep His part of His eternal promise, and even assuring our place in the relationship, if we choose to continue to stay strong in our faith (Jeremiah 31:31-34). Jesus came to be the fulfillment of God's promise, so that we would have the power to accomplish His will.

God actually experiences great sorrow for us when we don't live the way He knows is best for us (Ephesians 4:30). Sometimes, we think that He is so 'big' that He can handle whatever we have to dish out. But while He really *is* that mighty, we often fail to see Him as the tender hearted Father that He is – and our intimate friend. We often hurt Him without giving it a second thought. But thinking of our Lord suffering because of our disobedient behavior might motivate us to improve our commitment to holiness.

As we come to understand and trust God's faithfulness and provision through our trials and experiences, it will become evident that God is *able* to keep His part of the agreement NO MATTER WHAT, because He can see every moment in eternity. There are never 'extenuating circumstances' by which He will ever fail His part of any agreement (Psalm 105:8). He is not weak, and He cannot lie (Titus 1:2 and Hebrews 6:18). He doesn't get too tired, nor does He sleep (Psalm 121:4). He never changes (Psalm 102:27; Hebrews 13:8 and James 1:16). He is all-powerful and is **able** to keep His Word, which is absolute Truth (Psalm 145:6). And there is *nothing* in His character that will deter Him from accomplishing what He says He will do. Our job is to **believe** Him.

Benefits of keeping our word

So, what are the benefits of keeping our commitments?

- We have a clear conscience
- We build a good, strong reputation
- We are stronger each time we follow through
- We please the Lord
- We benefit other people
- We train our children how to be responsible

Another amazing benefit of *staying* committed to God is that He will increasingly give us the desires of our hearts (Psalm 37:3-5). This is the result of our relationship with Him – He changes our hearts and minds so we begin to *want* the things He wants. Then, He can really answer our prayers, because they are in alignment with HIS will. We still have to wait for His timing, but many of our godly prayers will be answered

(James 5:16). When we **commit** our ways, our plans, and our lives to Him, He promises to help us through life (Psalms 37:23-24). When we trust in Him with our whole being, He also promises to direct our steps (Proverbs 3:5-6). As God's Spirit works through us in this intimate relationship, our old behavior supernaturally changes, and we begin to experience new thoughts, feelings, and values.

Personally, I *want* God to show me the way, because He is the only One who can see my future. He has known me from the foundation of the world, and He *already* knows what is going to happen to me! Since He created me in my mother's womb (Psalm 139:1-17), He knows how I will operate to my best potential. God has used countless circumstances in my life to prove that He is REALLY there for me. And I continue to choose to rely on the commitment He has shown me in the past, as I believe in the hope He promised me for my future.

<u>How can I become more committed?</u>

How do we learn to be a committed people? Well, our commitment to God will stay constant and alive if our devotion comes from a soft, compliant heart. This is 'active love'. It means that we make a conscience decision to offer ourselves to Him and others. You may not realize it, but our hearts actually grow in devotion the more we 'chase' after the Lord! Besides, He <u>deserves</u> our adoration, and praising Him literally changes our minds, our hearts, and our focus (Psalm 145). And we can develop this loving response to our God by:

Reading and obeying His Word

Prayer

Spending time with other, like-minded, uplifting, genuine believers

And devoting ourselves to service to others.

- Stop here to examine your daily routine. On most days, how much time do your spend in the Bible? In prayer?
- How much time do you spend with other positive, godly Christians?
- And how much time do you spend per week helping someone outside of your family or your job?

This exercise is not to guilt trip you – it's to help you discover your values so that you can realign them so they will honor God. It certainly is not easy to change our lives, but it is SO rewarding!

Scriptures to strengthen and transform your character

Commit our work to the Lord	Proverbs 16:3
Entrust our habits, sins, attitudes, and behaviors to the Lord	Psalm 37:5
Entrust our spirits to the Lord	Psalm 31:5
Commit ourselves to His Truth (which means staying obedient even in the face of opposition)	1 Timothy 3:9
Commit our worries to Him	1 Peter 5:9
Understand that our *total* commitment to God is what He wants	2 Chronicles 15:14-15
As we commit ourselves to Him, He will bless us with peace	Isaiah 26:3-4 and 48:16b-18
Let Him renew our minds by His Word, the Bible	Romans 12:2 Hebrews 4:12-13 2 Timothy 3:16-17

Start by taking the time to devote yourself to God on a regular basis. Separate yourself from your routine, the phone, the computer, other people, and any other distractions. Choose to spend time renewing and feeding your relationship with Him. Recommit yourself to HIS purposes.

This is the way we have our character and hearts changed. Our devotion time is when we can truly be refreshed from the world and its demands. This is *especially* important when we think we are 'too busy' and don't have time to do it (Joshua 24:14-26). It might be difficult to discipline yourself in this way at first, but if you stick with it, you will find it becomes easier and more fulfilling with time. You will eventually wonder what you did before you set this time aside with Him. And you'll feel less complete if you miss these new opportunities to be with Him.

- Write down 3 practical ways you can get away to be with the Lord during the week. Maybe you can swap a job, babysitting, or housework. You can take a drive away from the house. You can get up a half an hour earlier before the family is up. If you want this, you *will* find a way!

Jesus does not mince words about following Him. We need to get rid of any obstacles in our lives that interfere with obeying Him. As God's Son He has the absolute right to demand complete loyalty from us (Matthew 16:24-28). **Nothing** should be placed above our commitment to living for Him.

It is only as we make these choices with His Spirit's help that we will understand how fulfilling the Christian life really is (Matthew 10:38-39). When we pledge our *whole* life to His service and His plans, we will discover the real purpose of living. We will find true stability, satisfaction, and healthy self-esteem. So, make a promise today to become more committed to God, yourself, and others! You will never regret your decision.

Half-hearted commitment is worse than no commitment at all

REFLECTION

1. What are some areas in your life that you need to work on your commitments? Maybe it's making less commitments, more commitments, or actually following through on your commitments.

2. What are some areas in your life that you are very committed? This may be your relationships, your job, your marriage, your kids, or your church. What is your motive behind your commitment in each situation? (love, money, guilt, prestige, reputation, etc).

3. Now, on a scale from 1-10, write down how important each of the above commitments are to you. Be completely honest.

4. Now, consider your 'very committed' areas. Are they in alignment with the will of God for your life? In other words, do your **priority** commitments center on God and His kingdom? And helping others come to Christ? Are they centered on becoming more intimate with Him? If not, why not?

5. We all have 'mundane' commitments in life, and they are a necessary part of living in this world. However, the way to examine our lives to see if our commitments are **in a godly order** is to honestly look at our actions. What are we spending our time, money, and talent on? And are we changing – becoming more loving, less irritated, more giving?

6. Think about your commitments: Are you just running around 'busily' – feeling like you are 'accomplishing' a lot, but in reality, the things you are doing are shallow and not really helping anyone? Write down how important these activities are in the light of eternity. Will they be relevant when you meet Jesus (Matthew 25:31-46)?

NOTES

DISCIPLINE

What do you think of when you hear the word discipline?

Do you think of an angry God who does nothing but sit around and wait for you to do wrong, so He can punish you? Does it bring to mind feelings of pain? Dread? Do you feel stifled, inferior, or anxious when you hear that you are going to be disciplined? Maybe you have never been disciplined, and you don't really know what it is. Or perhaps you were 'kept in line' by an abusive parent who 'disciplined' improperly.

Let's get started by taking a look at what the Bible says about this powerful and necessary function: Discipline.

<u>We're adults, so why do we need discipline?</u>

The Hebrew word for 'discipline' means to 'chastise with blows or words, to correct, instruct, train, teach, or reform'. God wisely calls us His children, because just as a child needs their parents' influence, we need the Lord to guide us, lead us, and direct us if we want to live healthy, godly lives. And when we are not living according to His standards, we need to be brought under His corrective hand.

When God feels we need to be disciplined, He will allow us to go through uncomfortable and even painful circumstances to bring us to a place of humility. Humility is not humiliation, but rather an attitude that leads us to admit our dependence on Him.

Contrary to what we may believe, He allows these trials because of His LOVE for us (Hebrews 12:6). This scripture goes on to say that if He didn't discipline us, we would be considered *illegitimate* children (Hebrews 12:7-9). Our discipline from the Lord is always delivered in His perfect way, as it is never delivered in anger, frustration, or on the spur of the moment.

We also find that He corrects us so that we can *share in His holiness* (Hebrews 12:10). What a privilege to be partners in the nature of Almighty God! As we follow His ways and plans, we become more like Him, because as we choose to turn from our disobedience, the Holy Spirit will feel more and more 'at home' in our lives. God wants us to live a righteous life so that we can experience the fulfillment of His purposes. Far from being a cruel and unjust taskmaster, God wants the best for us, and He will use difficult situations and people in our lives to accomplish the refinement He knows we need. And while it's true that He gives us free will to ignore His chastisement, the consequences are grave (Proverbs 15:10).

- Do you think you are too good, or too old, to be disciplined? ☺

Rebellion

The opposite of living a life of spiritual discipline is *rebellion.* The Hebrew translation for rebellion is 'to make bitter; to sin grievously, or to revolt'. It is basically saying that I *will* do what I want, no matter what God has to say. Pride and rebellion are bedfellows; if you have one, the other is sure to follow. 'Pride' says that I can live my life apart from the power of God and I am the only person who really matters. Remember, this is precisely what got Satan kicked out of heaven (Isaiah 14:12-14), and God is no less happy about these attitudes in us today.

The Bible says that obedience is the key to God's heart, but rebellion is as bad as **witchcraft** (1 Samuel 15:22-23a). Early in the Bible, God strictly prohibited this practice (Leviticus 19:26 and Deuteronomy 18:10-14). When we consult anything other than the Lord to guide our decisions or our future, we are really saying that God is not wise or important enough to direct us. And when we reject God's advice, the Bible says we are literally *stupid* because we hate correction (Proverbs 12:1).

We also open ourselves up to demonic forces when we seek knowledge or wisdom through any source except from the God of the Bible. Incidentally, astrology (not the study of stars, but the way people use this to determine their destinies) and horoscopes fit into this category. If you are 'reading' your horoscope, using tarot cards, playing with ouija boards, or anything like it – STOP. These pastimes are truly satanic in nature. What may seem innocent enough is really opening us up to 'divining', an old practice that uses magic and the occult for insight, rather than searching for wisdom from God (Deuteronomy 18:10-14).

- What are some practices you use to gain insight and wisdom in your life that are not from godly sources?

<u>Self-Discipline</u>

If we were raised with a lack of discipline while growing up, we can easily carry our unhealthy attitudes and habits with us into adulthood. We may try to get our own way no matter whom we hurt. We may be so spoiled that we continue throwing tantrums when life doesn't go our way. Besides being a pain to be around, these old behaviors can adversely affect the relationship we have with God and others. When we live as though no one else matters, we'll try to manipulate or pout when we want something. We then become irritated when our prayers are not answered the way we want.

But remember, we are children of the Lord, and as such, we need to be told 'NO' at times! When we disregard others by our lack of self-control, we fail to make positive boundaries and end up hurting ourselves and others. The Bible says that "a person without self-control is like a city with broken down walls" (Proverbs 25:28). Since we don't have walls around our cities today, we may think this is a ridiculous proverb. But in biblical times, cities had very high and very thick walls for protection; if their walls were not secure, they were in danger of losing their belongings, their city, and their very lives.

We can liken these walls to the healthy limits we set in our lives. When we refuse to control ourselves, we actually become vulnerable to attacks from the enemy. Insecurity is common, because there is no standard by which we compare ourselves, and we have no basis for right and wrong. Just like a fence that has been broken, a lack of boundaries fails to keep the negative influences out of our lives, and at the same time, it also fails to protect us.

While living according to our own feelings, thoughts, and desires may seem pleasurable at the time, the truth is that we were created to want and need moral, physical, and spiritual boundaries in our lives. When God corrects us, we are meant to learn self-control through the process of intentionally bending our will to His. We may think of self-discipline as an impossible achievement that lacks pleasure and excitement. But we will find that when we learn to control ourselves through the power of the Holy Spirit, we will experience feelings of accomplishment. As we learn to train ourselves to behave in the way God prefers, this will bring a sense of well being into our lives. And genuine, eternal fruit comes from a life that is submitted to, and controlled by God.

- What are 2 areas that you could use more self-control?

Are you resisting the Lord's correction?

People often think that by 'obeying all the rules', they will escape God's chastising. Many religions in the world are based on an 'outward appearance' philosophy. They think if they 'go through the actions' of being nice, going to church, and helping the elderly across the street, they will fool God and others. They might even cry "Why am I going through this, God? I thought was doing everything right!" They become resentful when they face hardships, because they believe that their outwardly 'good' behavior is making up for their lack of heartfelt, pure devotion to God (Matthew 23:25-28). While Jesus is actually talking to the religious leaders of the day, the concept is exactly the same for us when our motives do not line up with our behavior.

God chastises us when we 'fake' the Christian life, because His desire is to have our hearts softened so that we obey Him out of our *love* for Him, not because we *have* to. Our propensity to keep rigid rules or rituals does not make Him love us any more than He already does. As a matter of fact, we deeply offend Him with this kind of behavior. While God is absolutely delighted when we desire His will and walk in His ways, He deeply and steadfastly loves us exactly the same, no matter *how hard or how seldom* we try.

We tend to hide from God when we know we are at fault. But the longer it takes for us to come to Him, admit our wrongs, repent from our self-centeredness, and start following His ways, the longer we will go 'round and 'round with Him until we either harden our hearts and reject Him, or we yield to His correction and modify our lives so we behave more like Jesus.

- What are 2 areas of your life that you are in process of yielding to God?
- What are 2 areas that you are rejecting God and following your own desires?

Genuine freedom

God created us in His image, and until we are living the life He has outlined in scripture and through the wisdom of His Holy Spirit, we will never feel true satisfaction. Just looking around at our society proves that living only for our 'self' results in anxiety, instability, and depression. As we see a decline in the morals and discipline in our nation today, we see chaos escalating everywhere.

Many people think that God is 'all about the rules and regulations'. But again, His **love** is the motivating force behind all He does (Revelation 3:19). Like a wonderful parent, He wants us to stay away from things that will bring us self-induced hardship and pain. The reality is, if God had no standards of right and wrong, we would fail to respect Him. And while we may feel discomfort during a time of discipline, we are never safer and more loved than when we know our Father is in control and cannot be shaken. I take comfort in the fact that God cannot be irritated, manipulated, or distracted by my foolish or selfish ways.

Remember, we are always 'free' to sin. But that is not genuine freedom. It is enslavement to our flesh. It is only as we allow God's Spirit and power to strengthen us to overcome our old desires that we are truly liberated.

- Would you say you obey the Lord out of love or fear?

Scriptural discipline

The Word of God has plenty to say on the subject of discipline. For additional study, I suggest you take your personal devotion time to meditate on these scriptures. You can also look up the references listed next to the following Scriptures in your Bible:

- Do not to ignore the Lord or get discouraged when you face His correction, because He is actually showing His love for you (Proverbs 3:11-12)
- Fear of the Lord is the foundation of true knowledge, but fools despise wisdom and discipline (Proverbs 1:7)
- To learn, you must *love* discipline; it is stupid to hate correction (Proverbs 12:1)
- Fools think their own way is right, but the wise listen to others (Proverbs 12:15)
- There is a path before each person that seems right, but it ends in death (Proverbs 14:12)
- Those who follow the right path fear (are in awe of, and respect) the Lord, but those who take the wrong path *despise Him*
- Turning from God brings destruction (Proverbs 1:28-33)
- The wise are glad to be instructed, but babbling fools fall flat on their faces (Proverbs 10:8)
- People who accept discipline are on the pathway to life, but those who ignore correction will go astray (Proverbs 10:17)
- If you reject discipline, you only harm yourself, but if you listen to correction, you grow in understanding (Proverbs 15:32)
- God's Word is the blueprint for our lives (Proverbs 6:23)

<u>Healthy discipline</u>

Wholesome discipline is beneficial when administered fairly, quickly, firmly, and lovingly. In addition, beneficial discipline *always* involves healthy boundaries. If it is administered correctly, it puts the interest of the one being disciplined first. Far from being a reason for despair, obedience and self-control results in a life of vitality, encouragement and perseverance. This is the pattern the Lord uses with us, and it is the pattern by which we should raise our children. More is said about disciplining our children in the 'Disciplining our Children' study in this book.

- Can you think of a recent situation where you went through hardships or discipline because of your sin or poor choices?
- How did you feel during your trial? Did you feel like a 'bad' person, or a loved child?
- Do you believe that you matured during this time?
- Did your relationship with God grow closer or farther apart?

<u>Who you hang out with is who you become (Proverbs 13:20)</u>

Because others influence our thoughts and behavior, our ability to be self-disciplined and to live godly lives will be greatly affected by the people we spend time with. When we become Christians, we will probably still have friends who have not made a decision for Jesus. But one of the biggest mistakes new Christians make is trying to keep these old relationships alive. If your old friends are living any type of immoral lifestyle, it is very important that you begin to distance yourself from them. While we should try to influence others for Jesus, we need to spend the majority of our time with believers who are living an authentic Christian walk. It may be hard to imagine, but old friends who are unsaved will likely pull you back to your old life before you bring them to Christ.

At the same time, if we are sincerely seeking Jesus, we usually find that the ungodly people we used to spend time with will no longer hold the same appeal as they did before. The behavior we used to think was amusing will seem very inappropriate now. Instead, as we become more like the Lord, we will instinctively be drawn to those who exhibit the fruits of the Holy Spirit – positive, hopeful, and healthy people. This is not to say your old friends are necessarily bad, but our new life in Christ should result in morals and values that are different enough to make us uncomfortable around ungodly talk and behavior.

Again, choosing healthy, godly people to surround us in our new life is essential to our Christian growth. It is often difficult to release ourselves from these friendships, but it is essential if we want to grow in our faith. This is not a 'secret society' or an 'us and them' mentality. Rather, it is meant to preserve our life-changing attitudes, thoughts, and behaviors.

- Do you have any friends you spend a majority of your time with that may not be good for you in your Christian walk?
- Are you willing to let go of them for Christ's sake? (Matthew 10:34-39)

<u>What are the benefits of discipline?</u>

Believe it or not, *joy* is a significant benefit of allowing God's discipline in our lives (Job 5:17 and Psalm 94:12). Similar to relationships in a family, when disobedience is dealt with by discipline, attitudes are corrected and relationships are restored. And it's exactly the same with our Heavenly Father. As He brings us in line with His will through discipline, and as we choose to live according to His Word, the sweet fruit of restored relationship is ours when we obey.

We also find that we will reap *a harvest of right living* if we accept His discipline (Hebrews 12:10-11). I used to think that breaking the rules and 'doing my own thing' was fun. After all, I was just 'being myself'! However, after years of this kind of living, I came to the end of myself and found I was ready for something much more than selfish, empty days, self-hatred, and a hopeless future.

When I became a Christian, I learned that I was created to live in the shadow of the Most High God (Psalm 91). My life was meaningless apart from being in relationship with the Lord. I realized that I wasn't fulfilling my God-given purpose in life, because I was following my own path. And the strange thing was, I didn't even know that I was drifting on the sea to nowhere. I just knew I was miserable.

As we go through the trials of discipline, we learn more about ourselves, because fiery testing shows us what we are really made of (Psalm 119:65-80). We learn new boundaries and find increased stability when we trust the Lord through our trials and hardships. And we'll find that the more we lean on Him, the stronger we will become (2 Corinthians 12:9-10).

We may find it very hard to obey God in the beginning of our Christian walk, or after a season of rebellion. Change is always difficult, but don't give up! We all have a hard time turning our desires, choices, and plans over to anyone but ourselves. But as we get to know God's character and His ways, it will become easier to learn to submit ourselves to Him, because we will learn that His discipline and leadership is always loving and right.

Life-changing power

The good news is that no matter how we have been raised, or how we are living right now, Christ's power can completely change our lives. As we turn our wills over to *His* plans and purposes, He will give us the power and the desire to take control of our own emotions, actions, and thoughts, which will equip us for productive service in His kingdom (Philippians 2:13). As we allow the Holy Spirit to mold us, we will find we need less correcting. Our desires will change and we will increasingly crave God's ways instead of our own. And this will bring us what we have truly been looking for - genuine and lasting joy, peace, hope, and stability.

REFLECTION

1. Do you believe that you need God's occasional discipline?

2. What is rebellion?

3. What attitude always accompanies rebellion?

4. Do you tend to hide from God when you are disobeying? (hiding can come in the form of ignoring our sin, justifying and rationalizing our sin, or even staying away from church, the Bible, and other Christians).

5. Do you fear the consequences of your sin more than you fear hurting the Lord with your sin?

6. List 3 close friends or family members that you suspect may be damaging or hindering your relationship with God.

7. List 2 ways you might start to distance yourself from them.

NOTES

DISCIPLINING OUR CHILDREN

This study will be more helpful if you have already done the previous study on God's discipline for adults. Much of the discipline we receive from the Lord is a model that we should use when we discipline our children. And as we come under the correcting hand of God in our lives, we will begin to live as shining examples of obedience and holiness to our families.

Disclaimer!

I would like to begin by saying that I was certainly not a good parent in raising my own children. Only by the grace of God have those relationships been restored. However, over the twenty two years that I have been a child of God and have been the recipient of His loving discipline, I believe I *understand* how He would like us to parent our children. His Word also gives us a plethora of information from which I have written a good portion of this study.

In addition, you may have strong opinions about this study, and some of you may outright reject its truths. Some of the words used in this study may not sit well with you, either. We have been so lulled by our society into a 'politically correct' vocabulary that we have stopped using certain words because others might be 'offended'. I have used old-fashioned words like 'discipline', 'spanked' and 'punishment'. You may feel the hair on your neck raise, but these are biblical words. And since God has not changed the meaning or the name of these words in His Holy Bible for thousands of years, I'll stick to His ways.

You may even feel somewhat defensive while reading this material, as we tend to do when other people try to tell us how to raise our own little Johnny or Susie. And our culture has brainwashed us to think we have to put our children first in our lives, and let them do what they want so their little personalities won't be harmed.

But if your child is lacking respect and self-control, I hope you will allow God to speak to your hearts through this study. I pray that you will benefit from God's timeless wisdom on this critical subject. Our job as Christians is to align ourselves with God's ways, not to stubbornly look the other way or refuse to change. Even if you are not of the faith, these truths are valuable.

Since there is a section on spanking, I would like to say before we begin that many people do not believe in spanking. I have found that most people want to be good parents, but they often fail to raise their children biblically, only because they do not know how. Today, mom and dad almost have to be given 'permission' to retake the position of authority in their child's life. And some parents think they can correct their children by *explaining* to their two and three year old why they shouldn't be acting the way they are. The truth is, many children at that age are too mentally and psychologically immature to really understand this form of training.

Finally, there certainly are children who do not need to be spanked when they need discipline, so obviously, you don't need to spank your child if it's not necessary. Sometimes, a 'look' or a word can do the trick. But for most children, there will come the occasional situation when a healthy spanking is in order. And if you have a particularly willful child, then the following study has wonderful truths from God's Word that will help you regain a peaceful home.

So if your children are stable and well behaved, my hat is off to you. Maybe you can share this study with one of your friends who are having trouble understanding how to train their children 'in the ways of the Lord'.

Let's begin by doing a brief self-assessment on our parenting skills:

- Write down what kind of parent you think you are. You can use words like liberal, permissive, moderately strict, overbearing, controlling, etc.
- Now, consider your children. Are they well-behaved, pretty undisciplined, or are they ruling (and ruining) your household?

The beginning of liberal child-rearing

Doctor Spock seems to have had it all wrong. He taught that we should use every method except for corporal punishment (spanking) to discipline our children. Other like-minded psychologists teach us that our little children have very sensitive egos, and to use any form of boundaries or punishment will just crush their spirits.

However, it just takes a quick look around our society to see that this shift from biblical child-rearing to passive parenting has not produced good fruit in a good majority of the children. Of course, there are some really great kids out there, but we are going to discuss some of the ways our society has undermined and weakened the biblical ways of child-rearing, which have even influenced Christians in the process of raising their kids.

What does the Bible say about disciplining my child?

Are you ready? Proverbs 19:18 says *we will ruin our children's lives* if we don't discipline them. WOW! When we fail to discipline our children, we are setting them up for difficulties for the time when they will need to submit to the Lord. We see a serious lack of respect for authority in our culture today, and even less regard for God. Verse 23 says that respecting God gives us life, security and protection from harm. No wonder people feel so restless, vulnerable, and fearful today!

The Bible says that the fear of the Lord is the beginning of wisdom (Proverbs 9:10) and that fools despise wisdom and discipline (Proverbs 1:7b). 'Fear' of the Lord does not mean a state of terror, but rather to have a 'healthy respect' for Him. Just as we need to have this well-adjusted attitude of awe for God, our children need to be taught to have a certain amount of fear, or respect with their parents. When we discipline our kids in a loving, firm way, we instill this attitude into them.

Remember when you were young – did you fear being grounded or losing television privileges? No! But if dad was on his way home and you knew he would spank you for what you did – now THAT was scary! Chances are, if we were raised with this kind of healthy fear, we ended up respecting and loving our parents even more, because they were brave enough to stand up to us and place those essential boundaries around us. They taught us self-control, and most likely, we felt a whole lot more loved and secure than if we were allowed to do anything, or act any way we wanted.

It is always unpleasant for the parent and the child when punishment needs to take place. However, just as it is necessary for an adult's character development when God deals with our waywardness, so it is for our children when we discipline them. When our children are out of control, we **rob** them of the experiences they need in order to build strong character. They will grow up becoming weak and foolish instead. And this will cause them to sow discord, or conflict in the home, which the Lord *hates* (Proverbs 6:16-19).

Proverbs 19:26 says children are a disgrace when they disrespect their parents. And how true that is! How many times have we seen a spoiled child in a store or restaurant? They cry and scream for their way, and usually, the parents are so embarrassed, they give in to the child's demands. What the child needs is to be taken out to the car and firmly told "No". If that does not work, a well timed spanking may be in order to train the child to control himself.

Children often act out in an attempt to have the parent take control

Nowadays, I hear parents asking their children what they want to eat, what they want to wear, what they want at the store, and where they want to go. It seems they want their children's input on every decision. While children should be given some say in family matters according to their age and maturity, many decisions should just be made and carried out by the adults. Most of the time, children do not truly want the responsibility of making all of these decisions. They just want to be kids.

I repeat- children are too young and immature to run the lives of adults! As they mature, of course, they should be allowed to make more frequent, and more important choices. But a child's job is to grow up through critical stages in order to *become* decision makers. Little choices along the way are appropriate building blocks. But giving a child too much control is like someone turning over a Fortune 500 Company to the secretary and saying "Here, you manage it" - when they have had *no* previous training. That would be a ludicrous idea! But this is precisely what happens when we let our children constantly control us and our decisions.

Spanking

Proverbs 29:15 says that the rod of correction produces wisdom in our children, but a child left to himself is a disgrace to his mother. Verse 17 says the fruit of our discipline will be our happiness and peace of mind, as well as our children's. Proverbs 23:13 says that physical discipline may very well save their lives, and that it certainly will not kill them! Spanking is proper *as long as it is not administered too harshly, too often, or in anger.* The world's system has conned us into thinking we will damage our children if we spank them occasionally, or that it is considered child abuse.

While we're on the subject, we all know that child abuse exists. It is a horrendous crime. And I am certainly not advocating harming your child. But if you look up the laws of your state, you will likely find a clause that says something to the effect: "It is the parents' responsibility to have control over their children". There is permission to swat little Jonny "If it is not done as to cause long term physical or mental anguish". God's way of discipline results in honor, not horror.

I challenge you to a fun exercise. Ask 6 people over the age of forty if they were ever spanked. Now ask them if they feel they are mentally deranged or ruined for life as a result. Ask them if they felt their parents loved them because of this discipline. The truth is, we will probably not meet anyone who died from being spanked in a healthy way when they deserved it ☺. And likely, our interviewees will say that correction helped them avoid potential mistakes in their future, and taught them to respect their parents and other people of authority.

Does disciplining my children really matter?

Discipline has seriously declined in our society today, both in adults and children. We are bombarded daily with ideas that children should get everything they want. Television often portrays child insolence as funny and acceptable. There was a time when children used to address their elders respectfully, saying please and thank you. They did chores in the family and got a 'swat' when they needed one! Now I hear children disrespectfully ordering their parents around – and astoundingly - mom and dad are actually obeying! We have definitely lost our way.

We read in 1 Samuel 3:13-14 that we will be judged by God for the way we have raised our kids. The main reason the Lord is so concerned about this child-rearing issue is because if we use loving discipline to train our kids, we are preparing them to submit to God later in life.

Secondarily, as we train our children in godly discipline, they will gain control over their wills early on, so it will be easier for them to work within the guidelines of society as adults. Certainly, we have all seen unruly friends, family members, or co-workers. They act like children – and oftentimes you will hear that they were undisciplined while they were growing up.

Mapping out the boundaries

Just as we need to know what is expected of us from God, our children need to know what we expect of them. Since God is a God of order, He *created* us to want and need boundaries. One essential component of discipline is to be consistent with the boundaries we set for our children. God is consistent, firm, and loving; so we should also mirror this approach. Ideally, parents should initially sit down and determine some basic house rules, as well as the consequences for disobedience. The rules that are set need to be followed consistently, with only a small degree of flexibility. Don't worry if you haven't been training your kids well; anytime is a good time for new beginnings. But beware – you might want to start immediately, because the older they get, the harder it will be to introduce new habits.

Also keep in mind that rules are only effective if they are enforced. If a child lies one day and only gets a scolding, but the next time, gets grounded for a week, he will not only be confused, but he will become resentful. He will also become contemptuous of your rules because he knows they hold no power. If you feel uneasy about implementing rules in your home, it might help to compare our rules to traffic laws. They aren't there to keep us from having fun – they are there to protect our lives and help us feel secure. However, the traffic light means nothing if it does not carry a penalty for disobeying it. The same idea applies when we put the time and energy into teaching our children how to behave.

What happens if I don't discipline my children?

1 Kings 1:6 says if we do not discipline our children, they will not know how to work within the limits of home or society. This creates a spoiled, self-centered child who has no self-control and will actually be stunted in their growth. Teaching our children self restraint now will save untold misery in your future and theirs. When the child is misbehaving, it may seem like a 'cute' behavior now. But it will certainly not be funny when that child grows up.

Of course, there are certain behaviors that all children go through that are just part of growing up. They test our limits and get into trouble just to see what they can get away with. Part of this is normal and acceptable. They are learning who they are by testing their strengths and abilities in a safe environment. But when we excuse our children's willful disobedience or rudeness, we are doing them a disservice. When they are yelling at us, kicking, screaming, or being rude, we must not say "Oh it's just that age", or "That's just how Billy is – he has such a strong personality and he can't help it". By doing this, you are encouraging and accepting their rebellion. Instead, God's Word says that physical discipline can drive the foolishness out of a child's heart (Proverbs 22:15).

God says that rebellion is as dangerous as witchcraft (1 Samuel 15:23)! That is because rebellion stems from a hard heart and God cannot work with us when we purposefully reject Him because of our stubbornness. And this attitude starts when we are young. If we fail to train our children how to submit, we are teaching them that it is better to seek their own way instead of God's ways.

In addition, if we do not challenge our children to grow and become more self-controlled, they will lack the discipline and desire to attain high standards later in their lives. Rebellion will always be a part of the human condition, and we will battle it our whole lives. But we need to *train* our children in the Lord's ways. Children who are raised in a loving but firm environment are much more likely to be productive Christians and citizens as they get older. Human beings are like rose bushes. We grow better when we are pruned!

The parent trap

A common trap that parents get into nowadays is 'the guilt trip'. There are many forms of parental guilt, but some common ones include feeling remorse because we haven't been the best parents in the past. Or we may have gone through a divorce and we feel our kids have 'gone through enough already', and they don't need us to treat them negatively. Or our children are spinning out of control around us, and we feel terrible because we have no time or energy to correct them. We might have failed to discipline them completely, and now, they are throwing insults at us and we feel helpless to stop them.

Our child may truly be suffering from our lack of attention and discipline over the years, and are now using misbehavior in order to get attention. But the problem is compounded when we believe that if we are always 'nice' to them and let them do whatever they want, it will make up for the years of neglect. We may think that if we just give them everything they ask for, it will deaden their pain. Maybe we do nothing because we just don't want them to 'suffer' anything more. Or, heaven forbid, if we correct them, they may not *like* us. God's truth is that we *show our love* by carefully training and correcting them. It is at the very time they are going through hardships that they need firm boundaries in order to feel safe.

Just as we need to know that what we are doing is wrong and will not be tolerated from God or society, so it is with children. God put a conscience in each one of us, and if a child has no one to restrain their foolishness, they will cry out for someone to stop them. That is why we see so many children screaming and having tantrums in public. They are *begging* for someone to stop them – to help them feel secure. When we do nothing except for placate them in a soft voice or let them have their way, they still feel terribly insecure!

Another fallacy today is that we are our children's friends. Friends are at their mental and emotional level – they are peers. We are not their equals – we are their **parents**. We are designed by God to be their guardians, teachers, mentors, instructors, and examples. When our children are fully grown and their training is complete, *then* we can be their friends. If we get into this 'friend' mentality with them as they are growing up, we will lose the perspective of our responsibilities over them, especially when they need correction.

When we are in this 'friend' mentality', we will lack the ability to discipline them, because we don't want to hurt our 'friend'. We may not want to lose their 'friendship', and so we will be reluctant to reprimand them. And if we treat them as 'pals', they will certainly lose a certain amount of respect for us. Surely we should be 'friendly'! But we need to remember that we are in authority over them, and as such, we should be controlling their lives to a great extent. Just as God loves us intimately, but keeps a certain reserve because of His greatness and power, so it should be with our kids.

On the same note, we should be careful what we share with our children. While it is wonderful to have an intimate relationship with our children, many parents overburden their children with their problems. They also talk on the phone with their friends in earshot of the kids. Children are exposed to way too much adult information these days, and they are not mature enough to handle this level of knowledge.

They even become anxious when adult situations are shared with them. They don't understand the parents' anguish, nor can they do anything about it. We should not share our deep and personal struggles with our children – that is what *our* peers are for. Remember, wait until your kids are grown, then you can become the best of friends, and you can share your intimacy with them if they choose.

Tools to improve the way we administer discipline

One secret of healthy discipline is not to punish your children while you are angry. We cannot be sensible or fair when our own emotions are out of control. Wait until you have cooled down in order to address your child's misdeed.

Another helpful tool is to have your child tell you in *their* words what they did wrong. This helps them to understand exactly what they did. If they are young, you can explain to them what sin is and why it is harmful. When they get older, they will be able to identify the stubborn choices they made that clashed with God's will for their lives.

Additionally, if they have hurt someone, have THEM apologize for their behavior. It's not healthy for you to take the blame for your child's choices by saying you are sorry for their actions. Speaking for them takes away the sting of their misdeed. If they feel ashamed of their behavior, or are embarrassed to have to apologize, then they become much more sensitized to future sin.

Finally, after some time goes by and they have felt the impact of their actions and the consequences, it is very important to bring them close to you and tell them how much you love them. They need to know that nothing they do will cause you to love them any less. Teaching them about reconciliation will enable them to understand

God's forgiveness later on. This should be done before they retire for the night. Praying is a wonderful way to restore positive feelings, and it also helps them to learn how to turn to the Lord after they sin. If at this point, they do not want to be held, or are still feeling rebellious, let them be. They will miss your affection soon enough!

Practical pointers for loving but firm discipline

-Let the punishment fit the crime!

-Make sure the punishment follows quickly after the offense. This is especially important for younger children, as it is more difficult for them to associate discipline with the infraction if too much time passes.

-Make sure affection follows the punishment, but not too soon! They need time to feel bad about what they have done. But after an hour or so (less for small children), let them know you love them no matter what.

-Do not promise to punish and then fail to do it! This makes a liar out of you, and your children will ultimately disrespect your authority. Also, when you truly need them to obey you, they may end up ignoring you.

-Do not punish hastily or in anger.

-No bribes! There should be no reward for obedience except the satisfaction they feel because they have done the right thing. An occasional reward is fine, but don't let your kids expect treats every time they behave!

-No pleading!! We are the ones in authority over our children. I never heard the police begging me to obey the law! They punish hastily and surely when we deserve it, thereby earning the respect of society because of the way they dispense authority.

-As you are disciplining, talk to your child about why you are punishing them. As previously mentioned, allow them to state what it is they did wrong and why they are being corrected for it.

Example: "Shelley, do you know why I am giving you a spanking? If Shelley says "It's because she was a bad girl", then you can teach her how to define her sin by explaining "It is because you lied to Mr. Smith". The reason why it is important for your child to state their sin out loud is because it brings **healthy** conviction and shame. In time, Shelley will be able to verbally identify what she has done wrong by herself. Obviously, you will need to tailor the conversation to your child's age and maturity level.

-Teach your child how to make amends. You can tell Shelley "After we are done here, we will go next door and you can apologize for your lie". After that is done, and she has had sufficient time to think about her behavior, embrace her and tell her how much you love her. This process allows your child to feel healthy remorse and teaches them how to reconcile their feelings and relationships. In addition, it helps your child become accountable for his or her actions. They can see the important correlation between sin and its consequences. This also will help your child want to avoid this behavior in the future! Finally, it's important to remember that healthy, loving discipline will often be a powerful deterrent for our child's future sin.

<u>NOW is the time!</u>

If we have unruly children, we need to begin changing our methods immediately, because it truly gets harder by the moment! At some point, it will become impossible to restrain your child. We may not like it, but God's truth says that *if we spare the rod, we hate our children, but if we love them we are careful to discipline them* (Proverbs 13:24). Notice the word 'rod' is a physical tool that is closely linked to our love and commitment to our children. Lack of discipline means a lack of concern for our child's character development. Healthy discipline shows our loving protection and care. It takes great persistence and energy to train our children in the Lord, but it takes a lot less time and headache than if they grow up out of control.

God is the Perfect Parent. He has shown us through His Word and His character how to administer healthy discipline to our children. Remember, the relationship between us and our children is very similar to the one between ourselves and God. As we obey the Lord, our children will observe Who we turn to for wisdom, power, direction, and help. If they see their parents submit to God's higher authority, it will be easier for them to submit first to you, and then to Him. Pray with them! Show them through example that it is fitting to bring their lives under the control of our Father.

Children do not feel loved or safe when they are allowed to do anything they want.

REFLECTION

1. What are five essential points when it comes to disciplining our kids?

2. Name one thing that is attractive about a spoiled brat whose parent does not discipline them.

3. Write down five "fruits" that come from healthy discipline of our kids.

4. Write down five consequences if we do not discipline our children.

5. Your children will love and respect you ***more*** if you correct them with a firm, loving hand. T or F

6. We don't have to discipline as much when we or our children are going through hard times. T or F

7. If we fail to discipline our children, the Bible says we do not love them. T or F

8. If our kids are feeling bad, it's okay to hold off on correction at this time. T or F

9. We are our children's friends, and as such, we should do things for them so that they will like us. T or F

NOTES

FAITH AND ACTION: THE INTIMATE RELATIONSHIP

Christian faith is evidenced by the way we act

It's hard to believe that all we need is 'faith' in order to have a close relationship with the Creator of the universe! It's equally difficult to understand that our faith is the basis upon which we will spend eternity in a place so astoundingly beautiful that our minds cannot even envision it. But God, in His eternal wisdom, chose to bring us to Himself through ways that seem foolish to the world (1 Corinthians 1:20-27).

<u>What exactly *is* faith?</u>

The word 'faith' is described as 'reliance, loyalty, and complete trust'. Faith can be used in many contexts, such as a simple belief that your car will get you to your destination. Or, you may have a more complex faith, having a steadfast trust in God, Whom you cannot see.

We find one of the best biblical definitions of faith in the book of Hebrews. It says: "Faith is the confident assurance that what we hope for is going to happen. It is the evidence of things we cannot yet see" (Hebrews 11:1). God gave us His written Word because He wants us to know Him. He wants us to learn how to live our lives according to His principles. The Bible reveals to us where we will be after death, so we will have hope for the hereafter. Biblical faith is displayed by our trust that God will love us, direct us, protect us, and empower us, no matter what our circumstances. This is the type of faith that God wants every Christian to experience.

The Bible says "It is impossible to please God without faith" (Hebrews 11:6). Our faith literally determines the kind of relationship we will have with the Lord. Most of us realize after we come to the Lord that our 'spiritual eyes' were closed before we BELIEVED (1 Corinthians 2:13-16). We were unable to understand the principles that Jesus spoke of because they seemed so contrary to our human wisdom.

But once we place our hope in Christ, His Holy Spirit begins to allow us the understanding to see in another dimension. Upon salvation, our spirits literally become 'alive' through supernatural transformation. As a result, we receive and comprehend a new awareness in the spiritual realm. Faith is the reason why we believe that Jesus is alive and working in our lives, even when we can't see Him! The world simply cannot understand why we place ourselves in His hands, and why we live our lives according to His principles.

Coming to faith is not a one-time decision. Although it begins with our choice to accept Jesus, it continues to *grow* through a dynamic process. As we consistently decide to choose the Lord's ways over our own, we will begin to experience the 'abundant life' He describes to us in John 10:10. As we continue to remain in close relationship with Him, He shows us His faithfulness through every trial. Ultimately, we realize that He will remain true to His Word no matter what our circumstances. This is active faith.

- How would you describe your level of faith? Maybe you are just getting to know Jesus, and your faith is new. Or maybe you have been a Christian for a while, and your faith is lukewarm.
- Would you like to have more passionate faith?

Our Tower of Refuge

Faith has two components: Trust and Hope. *Trust* is the belief that God exists, and that He is Who He claims to be, as revealed in the Bible. It's the conviction that He is perfectly capable and dependable to meet our needs.

The word 'trust' is described in the Hebrew language as: '*To flee for protection and to hide for refuge*'. King David truly understood this when he wrote Psalms 91:1-2:

> Those who live in the shelter of the Most High
> Will find rest in the shadow of the Almighty
> This I declare of the Lord
> He alone is my refuge, my place of safety;
> He is my God, and I am trusting in Him.

And verse 4:

> He will shield you with His wings
> He will shelter you with His feathers.
> His faithful promises are your armor and protection.

This means that when we depend on God and believe His promises, He allows us to run into the shelter of His protection! It's the same idea as when you are sleepy on a rainy day and you crawl into bed. It's a warm, comforting place and a refuge from the world. It makes you feel like you are hidden away. This is the kind of experience that God wants us to have when we are trusting in Him.

- Who do you turn to when you are afraid?

Hope

The definition of *hope* is 'to wait, to be patient, to expect, or to anticipate with great pleasure'. When we have hope, it means that we believe God's **future** promises to us. This kind of hope includes the promise of eternal life with Jesus, the expectation of our new resurrected bodies, and the assurance of the joy we will experience when sin and suffering are done away with. Biblical hope doesn't mean that we 'hope' we get to heaven or we 'hope' God will keep us from suffering. It's a foundational mindset and attitude that we build our very lives upon, because we *know* the Perfect Object of our hope: Jesus Christ, the Faithful and True Savior (Revelation 3:14 and 19:11).

Those who have an intimate relationship with Jesus find Him to be *worthy* of their hope. He is steadfast, immovable, eternal, completely honest and absolutely trustworthy. This is definitely where I want my hope to be placed! I don't want to depend on this temporary, deceitful world, but rather on Someone Who doesn't change with time, weather, pain, emotion, or human frailty!

Many times in my life, it has been this very hope that has kept me going. I can see the victory line in my mind! Paul compared our earthly life in Christ to a race (1 Corinthians 9:24-26). Just as an athlete trains to win so he will receive a prize, so we need to keep our eyes on the confident assurance of seeing Jesus in heaven as our reward for faithfully serving Him (Matthew 25:23).

We often wish we could see into the future. But since 'hope' is *expectation* for the future, Paul reminds us that if we were given everything we long for right now, there would be no way to strengthen our faith, because we wouldn't have anything to look forward to (Romans 8:24-25). Yearning for something keeps us on track and gives us purpose.

- Do you have a solid belief that you are going to heaven?

Excuse **me**!

Excuses abound when it comes to our sin and our immoral lifestyles. Many people want to live by their own rules, and will almost viciously defend their 'right' to do whatever they want. When we reject God's ways and discipline, we will naturally want to blame others so we don't have to feel the embarrassment of our sin, or suffer the consequences for our transgressions.

And then there are those who consider themselves 'good' people, but they continually justify their reasons for not accepting Jesus Christ. I'm sure we have all run into people who say "I am a spiritual person and I have a spiritual walk. I believe in God, but I don't need to read the Bible or go to church to practice my faith". This is pure deception! Pride is at the root of this mindset, because pride says "I can run my life without God". Psalm 14:1 says "Only a fool says in his heart there is no God". Even if someone says "Oh I believe in God, I just don't want to have relationship with Him" – it's basically saying you don't trust God, so in reality, you might as well not even bother to believe He exists.

The Bible says that our hearts are deceitfully wicked (Jeremiah 17:9). It also says that there is a path that seems right to a person, but it ends in death (Proverbs 14:12). So you see, just because you 'feel' content living a 'spiritual life' without Jesus Christ, God makes it clear that if we aren't in relationship with His Son, we will not receive eternal life (John 17:3; Romans 5:1-11 and verse 21). In addition, we cannot live the life He intended for us apart from His Holy Spirit (Romans 8:5-11), and the Spirit is only available to those who have placed their trust in Christ (John 14: 15-21).

- What are some excuses you make for not serving Jesus more fully?

Where does my faith come from?

Now let's look at where our faith comes from. We read in Romans 12:3 that our faith originates from God, not ourselves. So we see that it is not our job to *obtain* our faith; it is our job to *receive* it. The Bible also says that faith comes from Jesus, who is also God (2 Peter 1:1). And there are times that God will give an *extra measure* of faith to people. This type of faith is an unusual gift of the Holy Spirit (1 Corinthians 12:9).

Romans 10:17 says that faith comes from hearing the Word of God, so our faith will continue to be refined and strengthened as we read the Bible and listen to biblical teaching. We also need to obey what we have learned from God in order to have our faith increased. It's pretty amazing that our faith comes from God, Jesus, the Holy Spirit, and the Word!

We find in scripture that it is essential to "test" ourselves to see if our faith is genuine (2 Corinthians 13:5). The way we do this is to examine our lives to see if we are growing. Are we less irritable than before we met Christ? Are we becoming more and more like Jesus, as outlined in 1 Corinthians 13:4-7? Are our bad habits decreasing with time? Do we desire a deeper relationship with Jesus as time goes by? Are we giving more of our time, energy, talent, and money to God's purposes?

If we are spending an inordinate amount of time on our own needs and ignoring others that need our gifts and talents, then our faith is not what it should be. Being a Christian involves active participation in helping others. It includes living in a way that brings glory to God. And it means *allowing* God to change our old thoughts, behaviors, and feelings.

The Christian life is not a system where we earn brownie points so we can gain more favor with God. But what we **do** for Him is a natural outflow of our love and devotion to Christ. As we press into God's Word and allow it to mold our thinking (Romans 12:2), it *will* result in a behavior change. Our values, morals, and goals will become different. We will begin to trust that God will meet our needs, so we can focus on giving our lives away to others (Matthew 6:31-34).

- What do you spend most of your time, money, and talent on?

Practical faith

Some important questions people ask are "How does my faith relate as I live in this world? What does it mean to live as a person of faith? And what's the point of having faith except to get to heaven?" James 2:14-26 talks about 'faith in action'. I'm sure we have all seen people who 'claim' to be Christians, but we know who they really are by the way they act (Matthew 23:23-28). While this scripture is referring to the religious leaders in Jesus' day, the spiritual principle is exactly the same for us when we say one thing and do another. *People with genuine, active faith in Jesus exhibit a likeness to Him.* And they go about doing good works because that is the ***fruit*** of their relationship with Him (Ephesians 2:10).

Another question people have about their faith is if their prayers really make a difference. Maybe you wonder if God is answering your prayers at all. We can get frustrated when what we have been praying for never comes to pass. The answer lies in the character of God. He alone possesses the power to see into the future, and as such, He knows what is best for us. Even though we think we have the best answer to our problems and we pray in that direction, the truth is, our solutions may not fit into the plans God has for that particular situation.

As an example, let's use our children. Your daughter asks if she can spend the night at her Christian friend's house. At first glance, that seems like a great idea! But little does your child know that just a few days ago, there was a terrible crime committed in that house. So, while her request seems good and innocent enough, you have the bigger picture, and you know better because you have more insight into the situation. It's exactly the same with us and God. He sees what future ramifications will come to pass when He allows our prayers to be answered. We <u>must</u> trust that He can see infinitely more than we can.

Maybe we've been praying for the salvation of a friend or family member and they haven't yet received salvation. That would definitely be the best of all prayers! In this case, we have to realize that the human will is the only thing that can stop God from acting. While we certainly *should* pray for barriers to be removed and for opportunities to be presented so that our loved ones can get saved, God will not force Himself on us.

This also applies to the area of healing. Many times, we pray for the healing of a friend or loved one, but God allows their suffering or death. We then feel that God wasn't listening or that He didn't really have the power to literally heal the person we prayed for. But again, we need to trust in the *character* and the almighty power of the God of the universe. His ways are completely different than ours (Isaiah 55:8-9), and He can see eternity at a glance.

I have witnessed many circumstances where someone's intense pain brought them to a place where they could accept Christ. I even know of people who have experienced motivation to change their lives after the death of a loved one. While we absolutely *ought* to pray for healing, we also need to let God be God. We need to come to know Him well enough that we will be able to rest in His final decision.

- Have you been praying for something that has not come to pass?
- Do you feel that God has let you down?
- Are you willing to let go of your plans and let God answer your prayers in His way and His timing?

You just don't have enough faith!

Maybe you're a Christian and you've been told "You just don't have enough faith and that's why your prayers are not being answered". This is unbiblical! There are many reasons why our prayers are not answered in the way we want. Our faith originates from God so we all have plenty of faith (Luke 17:5-6), even though some people's faith is weaker than others.

Another reason our prayers may not be answered is that we're asking for things that are not in our best interest (James 4:1-3). Or, we may have hidden sin in our lives that needs to be confessed and repented of before our prayers are heard (James 5:16-17).

We must be in intimate relationship with the Lord if we are to have His heart and mind. As we become more like Him through this union, our prayers will begin to change so they are more in alignment with His will. Then He will be able to answer our prayers (Psalm 37:4). When the desires of our hearts are changed, we won't care as much about the fancy cars, huge houses, and bigger bank accounts. Our new focus will be on other people – one's that are less fortunate than ourselves. We will start to ask for strength to help those in need. And THEN, God will be able to abundantly bless our prayers because we will be asking according to HIS will!!

Sanctification and Justification

Now that we understand why our faith is so important, let's take a look at what actually happens to our lives when we place our faith in Christ. The Bible says that we are actually 'set apart' from the world by our faith (Acts 26:18). The biblical word for this concept of 'setting apart' is called *sanctification*. It literally means 'to be continually cleansed and set aside for a distinct purpose'. Sanctification has two parts. If we have genuinely asked Jesus to be Lord of our lives, then our spirits are sanctified at the moment of salvation (Romans 5:16). That means if we died today, we would be with Jesus in heaven.

The other aspect of sanctification is an ongoing process. It involves disciplining ourselves so that our wills, thoughts, attitudes, emotions, and actions are continually being brought under the power of the Holy Spirit in our Christian walk. This is what it means when we hear the phrase 'dying to our flesh' (Romans 8:1-14).

We can 'see' the work of sanctification in someone's life by the fruit they bear (John 15:1-8). As born-again Christians, we *should* begin to look different from the world. We become distinctly different as God molds our lives to suit His purposes. We are no longer our own, because we have been bought with a price! (1 Corinthians 7:23).

Another amazing spiritual event that happens when we accept Jesus and declare our faith in Him is that we are *justified*. This means that we are made right with God and are placed in perfect standing with Him by accepting Christ's substitutionary death on the Cross. Jesus suffered and died so that we wouldn't have to. This is very good news to the believer, because it takes the responsibility off of our shoulders to reach perfect performance in order to please God, or to get to heaven. Which brings us to another subject……

No man is an island

Part of being in relationship with the Lord is living side by side with other people who have faith in Jesus. The truth is, we are not made to live our Christian walk by ourselves (Hebrews 10:25). God knew that we would need His Body, the Church, for support, teaching, and prayer.

And if we are trying to be 'good, spiritual people' without reading and obeying the Bible, we can easily get off base in our beliefs. Even Jesus explained the scriptures to His audience through preaching and teaching in a community of believers. Being part of the Body of Christ has nothing to do with being in a select group, the best club, or any other human institution. This IS all about what God has directed us to do in regards to our earthly and eternal lives.

Another common excuse I hear from people who don't go to church is "I don't do organized religion". Or "I've been hurt by religious people before, and I'm never setting foot in another church". The truth is, life will *always* be full of people who disappoint us and cause us pain. That doesn't mean we sever all relationships to avoid being hurt!

The church is made up of all sorts of people who are imperfect. Yes, some of them are even hypocrites! And don't forget, you have probably been hypocritical and hurtful to someone in your *own* life. We need to stop judging others – that's God's job (James 4:11-12)! Our job is to keep our eyes on Jesus, the Perfect One. He will never lie to us, cheat us, or gossip about us. He's the only One we can count on. If we all started loving each other the way Jesus has commanded us, instead of criticizing each other, we would have the harmony we so desire!

The bottom line is that God is the Final Authority. Since He made us with His own hands (Psalm 139:13-16), He alone knows how to direct our paths far better than any human wisdom we may be following. He paid for our debts and seeks to have an eternal relationship with us. Jesus Himself says "I am the Way, the Truth and the Life. No man comes to the Father *except through Me*" (John 14:6). We are treading on very dangerous ground if our 'spiritual' walk does not line up with the life God mapped out for us in His Holy Scriptures.

Consider the following scriptures:

- We can gather our thoughts (make up our own minds), but the LORD gives the right answer (Proverbs 16:1). *parenthesis mine*
- The Lord has made *everything* for HIS purposes (Proverbs 16:4a).

- We can make our plans, but the LORD determines our steps (Proverbs 16:9).
- God has planted eternity in the human heart (Ecclesiastes 3:11).

Our lives are the most fulfilled and purposeful when we relate to God as *He has ordained,* not as we have chosen. Indeed, we see that all paths **do not** 'lead to God'.

Off to work I go!

Most religions in the world require their subjects to strive to appease their gods. This 'work' often involves chants, human sacrifice, odd and sometimes brutal rituals, or severe self-limitations. These so-called 'religious' people involve themselves in 'holy wars' (oxymoron, huh?) and try to 'earn' enough points so they are in good standing with their gods. They go to great lengths so as not to offend their gods, and they live in constant fear of how their gods feel, since they believe their gods vacillate between anger and approval. They even kill those that do not believe in their god, all 'in the name of God'! And the only way they can determine if their god is happy is by the results in nature – good crops, healthy children, rain and sun, etc. These practices have been modified over the centuries, but the roots of these beliefs have been passed down through generations.

Even in America, there are plenty of religions where people have to do different kinds of service or rituals to please God. Sometimes, they have to bear many children so they will be 'represented' in heaven. Or, they are required to knock on their quota of doors. And they must bring in enough converts to their faith, in order to have done enough 'good works' to please God and earn their way to heaven. It is heartbreaking to see people wonder if they are doing *enough* to please God, and living in fear for their salvation every day.

However, the God of the Bible and Israel is fully delighted with us who trust in faith that *Jesus already paid the sin debt.* Our bill is paid up in full! He knew we would have never been able to earn enough to pay for our transgressions in our own power, so He lovingly did it for us. In fact, the Bible says "We are declared **righteous** because of our *faith*, not because of our works!" (Romans 4:5). While good works are a *result* of our relationship with Jesus, these works spring from our <u>love</u> for Him, not out of our <u>fear</u> that we're not doing enough to earn our way.

It is very important to *believe* what the Bible says about our salvation, as opposed to relying on how we may *feel* about it. Some days, we may not 'feel' very saved because we are struggling with sin. Or maybe we're going through a dark season and 'feel' that God is nowhere to be found. But as authentic, born again believers, we can rest assured in our relationship with God *because of our trust* in Jesus (Habakkuk 2:4; Romans 1:17; Ephesians 2:8-9; Galatians 3:11-12; and Hebrews 10:38). Because God is always truthful and does not change with circumstances (Hebrews 6:18), we can trust in His promises to remain true to us forever. And our salvation is secure as we continue to place our lives under His divine authority.

- Do you often feel that you are not measuring up to the standards of God?

<u>Faith and Action</u>

People can only see the supernatural work of God in our lives as we live a life controlled by the Spirit. When we exhibit love, joy, peace, patience, kindness, goodness, faithfulness, gentleness, and self-control, we exhibit behavior that reflects Almighty God! When we refuse to gossip, slander, or hurt others with our words and attitudes, then we are living righteously. And ultimately, when we go out of our way to help the poor and downtrodden, and use our time, money and talent to further the kingdom of God, then we are pleasing the Lord.

Don't think that people are not watching us - the world sees authentic Christian behavior as 'different'. People instinctively know that it is unnatural for humans to act this way! If we are consistently kind, generous, helpful, and joyful, we will then earn the privilege of telling those around us that it is the power of God in our lives that changes and motivates us.

About that fruit

We have learned that genuine faith is *faith that produces fruit*. This fruit includes sharing the gospel frequently with others as the Holy Spirit leads. It includes bringing glory to God every day, in whatever you do. It also includes ministering to the Body of Christ. And this fruit is *eternal* - it will last forever. Those who are attached to the Vine (Who is JESUS), bear much fruit, which brings glory to the Father.

Jesus says that every tree that does not produce good fruit will be chopped down and thrown in the fire (Matthew 3:10)! If you are foolishly building your life around your own selfish desires, you will be devastated when judgment comes (Matthew 7:21-27). The truth is, you are either serving yourself or the Master who is Jesus (Matthew 6:19-24). God wants fruit produced in our lives to bring glory to Himself, and to bring the lost into relationship with Him. God's primary concern is for people, and He uses those who love His Son to reach this unsaved world on His behalf.

Our faith is what sets us apart in this world. Christians are the only people in the world whose God is always available, all powerful, and eternally alive. He is the only one who loves us so intensely that He sacrificed Himself so we could be in relationship with Him. Our God is the only One who became a **servant** so we could become fellow heirs with the King for all eternity (Romans 8:17; Galatians 3:29; and Galatians

4:6-7). And He is the only God who never changes, never lies, never quits, never fails, and never dies.

Certainly, we have the freedom to make our own choices about our faith or our lack of it. But the Bible is clear that if we don't live out our faith according to the Word of God, we can easily be deceived into thinking life is all about us, our plans, and our 'religion' (2 Timothy 3:16-17) . If we reject the Person of Jesus Christ, we will eventually lose any spiritual truth we 'think' we might have had (1 Corinthians 4:4-5). Our minds will continue to be darkened and we will be unable to see His Truth at all (Ephesians 4:18-19). And in the end, there are only two places for us to go: heaven or hell (2 Thessalonians 1:9-12).

While God allows us to reject His ways, He Himself wrote the owner's manual for our life. Make no mistake: we will not get to heaven just by 'hoping' we will get there. Faith in Jesus is the <u>only</u> way.

****

Maybe you have never put your faith in Jesus. Maybe you are a Christian, but you don't have any fruit in your Christian walk. You might need to recommit your heart and life to Him so your relationship will be more intimate. Whatever the case, choose to serve Jesus more fully today. You will never be disappointed.

What we do for God is the only thing that will last forever

REFLECTION

1. What are some ways your faith is noticeable to the world?

2. What are a couple of things you could do to improve your actions so that your faith is more evident?

3. What are some areas in your life that you lack faith (hope and trust)?

    Money?

    Your children?

    Relationships?

    Your ability to change?

    Your future?

    Your ability to live a godly life?

    Your ability to share Jesus with others?

4. How do you know you have faith?

5. Can someone *act* like they have faith, but not really have it? How do we know?

NOTES

FORGIVENESS

Jesus said

"If you forgive those who sin against you, your Heavenly Father will forgive you. But if you refuse to forgive others, your Father will not forgive your sins" Matthew 6:14-15

WHAT?? How on earth am I supposed to forgive that evil person who caused me so much harm? Surely God is not expecting me to forgive *them*!!

<u>They deserve it!</u>

'Forgiveness' is kind of an old-fashioned concept today. When it comes to others sinning against us, it's much more likely you'll hear "I'm going to get back at them for what they did to me", or "I'm the one who was wronged – they need to say they are sorry before I even consider forgiving them". Or "I will *never* forgive them". But what does GOD say about forgiveness?

The above scripture from the book of Matthew sounds harsh, and actually impossible, until we really comprehend the overwhelming price that Jesus paid in order for *our* sins to be forgiven. In reality, we are completely without excuse for our sin – there

IS no defense for us regarding the way we act when we are out of relationship with God.

We need to remember that Jesus died for us *while we were still His enemies* (Romans 5:8). In essence, we were there when Jesus was being spit upon, bruised, beaten, and mocked. Jesus could have called His angels to annihilate mankind at that point. But instead, He *chose* to go through with the very sacrifice that would save Christians for eternity. Not only that, but His response on the cross was: "Forgive them, for they don't know what they are doing" (Luke 23:34).

It's unlikely that we will ever experience the suffering that Jesus endured on our behalf.

We are absolutely unworthy of His devotion, and we don't deserve His life sacrifice. And we only experience salvation, grace, and favor from God because of His *forgiveness*. The truth is, we cannot claim to be in an intimate relationship with the Lord if we continually refuse to forgive others, because each time we deny others mercy, our hearts are hardened. We not only shut the door of our hearts to the person we are refusing to forgive, but to God, as well.

We cannot begin to understand the kind of love that Jesus offered to us while He suffered, but we'll use an illustration here. Let's imagine that you are in a courtroom for the worst crime ever committed. Satan is the prosecutor, and he's spewing out ugly accusations about you (Revelation 12:10). On the other side, Jesus is your Defender (Hebrews 7:24-25), and God is the Judge. After Jesus has pleaded our case (Romans 8:34), God looks over the bench with eyes of complete love, compassion, and forgiveness, and says "You have been set free. What you have done will not be counted against you".

But He doesn't stop there. He continues "*I will have your Defender take the penalty you so richly deserve. He will suffer your consequences, and go through the pain, agony, loneliness, and shame so that you don't have to.* I only want one thing in return - your life devotion". When we see that this is precisely what Jesus did, we can understand why He calls us to forgive the lesser offenses that are committed against us.

Understanding the nature of forgiveness

First, we need to realize that **we cannot forgive in our own power**. Forgiveness only happens by supernatural means. Many of us try to live up to the standards in the Bible by our own efforts. And we have all failed miserably by doing this at one time or another, because God never intended for us to live out our Christian life alone. Many people have actually walked away from the faith for this very reason. They become so frustrated and burdened trying to 'act right', but they fail to use God's power to accomplish God's desires! The Lord sent us His Holy Spirit so that we *could* live life as outlined in the scriptures. *The power to forgive is only as strong as the relationship we have with the Lord.*

When we are continually in communion with Jesus, He gives us the power and desire to love others, and to carry out His will (Philippians 2:13). If we are controlled by the Holy Spirit, He will equip us so that we will be *able* to think and act in ways that please Him. When we place our trust in Christ, we will have His mind and His wisdom (1 Corinthians 2:16). Only then can we understand why He asks us to do humanly impossible things – like forgiving. But if we obey, we will be rewarded with a life of peace (Romans 8:5-6 and Philippians 4:6-7).

Another important thing to understand is that forgiveness does not have to be reciprocated. People will often remain the exact same way they were before we forgave them. Many refuse to forgive, because they think that forgiving someone means that the person that offended them will go unpunished. They feel like they are approving of what the other person did to them. But we must realize that God promises rest for

OUR souls if we obey Him in this matter. Living in Christ Jesus means that we *actively choose* to do what He has asked. And as much as we may not like it, we as Christians are responsible for making the first move towards forgiveness.

Finally, it helps to remember that forgiveness is a process. We don't just say "I forgive that person" and then instantly love them! More often than not, we will need to start by asking God for the DESIRE to forgive. And we might have to go through this process a hundred times. But each time we bow our wills before the Father and ask for His help to live His way, there will be a degree of healing and strengthening. Forgiveness is not a natural human response when we have been wronged! It takes time to heal from our wounds. However, if we submit to God's will by forgiving, we will find that one day we will no longer harbor ill feelings toward that person. And we will be free from the bitterness that consumes us.

- Are you willing to pray for the *desire t*o forgive those that have hurt you?

<u>We have access to the Throne room</u>

Because of the blood sacrifice of Jesus, the Bible says that we can come *directly* into the presence of God (Ephesians 3:12 and Hebrews 10:19-22). One way to understand the importance of this concept is to think of the kings and presidents here on earth. Do you think that you could just write the King of Spain and ask to spend a week in his personal palace? Or would you be able to call the Prime Minister of Australia on his personal phone, and talk with him for a couple of hours? Of course not!

But what's amazing is that we **can** talk to the Creator of the Universe (you know, the One who MADE the King of Spain and the Prime Minister of Australia ☺) anytime we want to. This is possible because Jesus Christ has brought us into right standing with God by paying the price for our sins. Because of this paid debt, we are considered 'holy' enough to enter God's presence (Romans 5:9-11).

It is also important to understand that through our relationship with Jesus, **God** is the One to forgive us – our sins are not absolved by any other human being. While we do receive forgiveness from others for our hurtful actions, our sinful *condition* can only be pardoned by the Lord. It is so comforting to know that as we come before God with a soft and sorry heart, our confession brings about His forgiveness (1 John 1:9). While confessing our sins to another person is important for healing and accountability (James 5:16), our direct contact with the Father brings true restoration and redemption.

We also find that, contrary to what many religions practice, the Bible clearly states that we do not have to go through a religious person in order to confess our sins to God (Hebrews 4:14-16). We have a unique benefit with our God that is not available in *any* other faith – because we have Jesus as our Mediator (Hebrews 8:6). That means He intercedes for us, and He prays to the Father on our behalf. That's why we say 'In the name of Jesus' when we end our prayers. Just thinking about the two of them talking about me brings me great joy!

As we begin to truly comprehend what happened at the crucifixion, we'll realize how important it is for us to allow the Holy Spirit to guide us through this area of forgiveness. If we are realistic, we will see that we have no right to hold onto previous grievances against us, when our Father has so graciously lifted *our* penalty. That is why Jesus linked our forgiveness from God to our forgiveness of others. He wants us to extend the very same kindness that He so lovingly bestowed upon us.

- Do you believe that God has truly forgiven you of your sins?

Our fortified walls

It's natural to defend ourselves from pain and attack. But if we continue to build walls around our feelings to keep from being hurt again, we disable ourselves. Our lives become brittle and unstable, because the old painful memories we have buried are always threatening to engulf us. We may be so afraid of our feelings that we cannot have real intimacy in any of our relationships. Remember, our walls may keep others out, but they also keep us imprisoned at the same time. Indeed, our protective mechanisms have the potential of robbing us of the ability to feel *any* emotions.

Our situation only gets worse when we realize that the walls we have built to protect ourselves are becoming less and less effective as we get older. Maybe we have a seething resentment about something that hurt us in the past. But instead of dealing with it, we find ourselves putting our 'masks' up– the mask of "I'm doing okay", or "I'm not mad", or "I'll make it through".

The problem is that if we use these masks regularly, we lose the ability to be honest with other people, because we are so busy deceiving ourselves in an attempt to hide the powerful pain or anger we are feeling. We may lose touch with ourselves as well, because we continue distancing ourselves from our true feelings in order to give the appearance that we have our lives under control. But our anguish needs a release, and we may find that we experience extreme pain or anger in situations that don't really seem that drastic.

Remember, God wants our healing even more than we do. And He promises to help us and keep us strong until death if we choose to stay in close fellowship with Him (1 Corinthians 1:8-9).

- Can you relate to any of the examples of the unhealthy responses listed above?

- What masks do you wear in order to give others the impression that you 'have it all together'?

Unforgiveness hurts *me*

Human beings naturally put up walls to protect themselves from being hurt. This is a perfectly normal response, and it can even be a healthy shield for a short amount of time. However, if we have had experiences in our lives where we've had to continually defend ourselves emotionally, mentally or physically, then it's likely that we'll need to revisit these painful memories in order to receive healing.

It's common to develop unhealthy responses if we've been hurt. People who have been put down, shamed, ignored or abused may display a variety of destructive coping skills. On the one hand, they may become very critical and condescending. These people think they are always right, and they don't let anyone get close to them. They rarely experience joy. They need to be exceedingly organized so they feel they have some semblance of control in their lives, because deep down, they know that their feelings are out of control.

At the other end of the spectrum are those who are completely passive. They let people walk all over them. They have little self-control or self-esteem, and talk openly with anyone about their past hurts. They seem to attract people who will take advantage of them or who will misuse them. These people have a tendency to feel guilty for mostly everything that happens to them in their life.

These are extreme examples, and we may fall anywhere in between. But the point is that living with resentment literally ruins our lives. If we continue reliving our old hurts over and over, they will eventually destroy us. We don't even realize that oftentimes, it's our unforgiving heart that drives our unhealthy desires, feelings, and actions. And our bitterness towards another person may be keeping us from nourishing relationships and a victorious Christian life. If you find that you are incapable of forgiving others, then you are actually a slave to your past, because you are chained to your painful memories. But the bottom line is, it's <u>our</u> choice if we are going to let God transform our hearts and minds (Romans 12:2).

We can only experience freedom when we forgive. Getting rid of the past will give the Holy Spirit more room to live and work in us. Allowing God to bring our pain to the surface so that we can be healed will most likely be a scary process, and it *will* bring some degree of suffering. But we can begin this process by asking God to help us deal with these issues. We might even need Christian counsel for support and direction. God promises that our lives *can* be restored (Joel 2:25), **but it is our choice.** Supernatural healing has happened in my life, and I have witnessed profound healing in others who have experienced terrible trauma in their lives.

- Do you think that unforgiveness might be one of the reasons you lack joy and peace in your life?

<u>Am I bringing honor to God?</u>

Genuine grievance begins with a sorrow for our attitudes. While we cannot deny that we have been wronged, God requires us to overcome our ill feelings. No matter what has been done to us, if we call ourselves followers of Christ, we are responsible to act and react in a manner that glorifies God. This does not let the other person who hurt you off the hook – they will answer to God for what they have done. But if we are honest, we will see that our own behavior of harboring bitterness and seeking revenge are not godly behaviors, either.

That is why God says "Vengeance is Mine" (Hebrews 10:30). He is the only One who has the right to confront and punish the people who have hurt us. Our job is to *obey*

His commands, not to judge others for their sin (Luke 6:37; Romans 2:1-4, 16; and James 4:11-12).

Additionally, when we choose to hold on to our unforgiveness, we grieve the Holy Spirit, because He cannot work in our lives when we harden our hearts (Ephesians 4:30). We <u>must</u> begin to forgive and start praying for the people who have offended or hurt us! The process of choosing to forgive others does not mean we have to rack our brain trying to remember every person in our life that did us harm. But if someone comes to mind that still causes you angry, hurtful, or negative feelings, you need the release of forgiveness.

God commands us to forgive, with a huge penalty if we do not, because He knows that the only way to spiritual, mental, and emotional freedom is through letting go of our pain and anger. We receive tremendous peace when we take our hands off the situation and let God do His job. Besides, He does it so much better than we do! ☺

- List some of the people in your past that still make you react negatively when you think of them.
- Make a commitment to begin praying for one person on your list every day for the first week. The second week, you can continue praying for them, and then add another person from your list. Even if you do not want to forgive someone, you can pray that God will change your heart so you *can* pray for them. Remember, they need Jesus just as much as you do!

<u>This is not fun</u>

Forgiving others who have deeply wounded or offended us will probably be a painful process. Any time we crucify our flesh, it will hurt! However, there are two kinds of pain – 'good' and 'bad'. The bad kind of pain leads to self pity and self loathing. When we choose to live as victims of our circumstances, we know deep in our hearts that nothing good can come from this type of pain. Many people who just 'let life happen to them' actually lack respect for themselves, because they know they are not doing anything to make their life better. God intended for us to overcome and be warriors in His kingdom!

The 'good' kind of pain is when we are suffering while we are growing or healing. Even though we may be hurting as we are being transformed into God's likeness, we are more likely to feel hopeful, because we know the end result of our trial will bring victory. And as we overcome our old, bitter feelings, we will see God's restoration in our lives. Unforgiveness crowds out the abundant life that Jesus talks about (John 10:10).

Finally, we need to be aware that as we are going through this time of growth, healing, and self-examination, our human tendency may be to try to 'do' something to avoid having to deeply face ourselves. We may find ourselves sleeping more, forcing ourselves to be involved in more activities, or avoiding solitude. This is called *denial.* The problem is that if we continue to resist God's command to forgive, we will find that our negative attitudes will begin to manifest themselves in other ways. We may find ourselves feeling increasingly sensitive, angry, judgmental, deceitful, indifferent, isolated, or depressed.

Do I have to forgive in person?

Maybe the person you need to forgive is deceased, or you don't know where they live. Or it might even be dangerous or unbeneficial to offer forgiveness face-to-face. While the ideal outcome for forgiveness is a mutually restored relationship, we will find that in some cases, this is just not possible. Additionally, if the other person is not living for the Lord, they probably won't have the capacity to forgive you, so you will be the only one in the relationship that is doing the forgiving. One way to get through this difficult time is to tell a trusted Christian friend that you are working on forgiving someone in your past. Ask them to pray for you and keep you accountable in your progress. In this case, forgiveness can happen in your quiet prayer time with the Lord.

Don't forget that you have also wounded people in *your* life, and you probably want the release of forgiveness yourself. We were created to need love, forgiveness, and restoration. The result of doing things God's way, even if it hurts at times, is that we become more like Christ. The truth is, we will never be the winners if we refuse to forgive – we will poison our relationships, instead. *We will continue to struggle in our Christian walk until we relinquish the 'rights' to our pain.* Think of it this way – we are going to go through pain in life no matter what – do you want misery and sorrow for it, or do you want a great reward? ☺

- Stop here and quietly ask the Lord to show you any obstacles that are keeping you from honestly facing yourself. Begin to pray about these issues so that you can be free.

<u>What if I refuse to forgive?</u>

We have learned that God has a real problem with our refusal to forgive. While our sins are forgiven because of Jesus' death on the cross, our relationship with God is tainted when we harbor unforgiveness towards other people (Mark 11:24-25). No matter how small or large the offense against us, our feelings of resentment or bitterness towards anyone ends the same – it produces an unhealthy crop in our lives. Unforgiveness is one of the most common reasons why we fail to walk in Christian victory.

You may be saying to yourself "I have forgiven everyone that has hurt me", or, "Those things are in the past – I have forgotten them". However, unless you have actually allowed yourself a time of reflection and examination on this subject, your old feelings are probably still part of your life. If you have trouble experiencing deep intimacy in your relationships, or you lack genuine, healthy self-love and self-esteem, bitterness may be the problem.

Maybe you are unable to commit to people or circumstances. Even for those who had a relatively 'good' upbringing, there are times throughout our lives that people have caused us harm, and we may still hold grievances against them, sometimes without even realizing it. While not all of us have 'unforgiveness boogeymen' in our closets, it's definitely worth thinking about.

- Is there someone in your life that you refuse to forgive?

Forgiving myself and God

One person we often overlook when we are contemplating forgiveness is *ourselves*. We may carry tremendous guilt because we have been the one to hurt someone in our past. Forgiving ourselves is a huge step to freedom. The truth is, Jesus died for our sins, and it would be arrogant for us not forgive ourselves since **He forgives us** when we genuinely repent.

One of the most common stories I hear in the area of self-forgiveness is regarding parents who have not been there for their kids while growing up. Many people allow this guilt to ruin their lives. We need to realize that if we have asked God for forgiveness, then we need to *let go* of the past and *let* Him heal our hearts. Remember, we can only do something about our present and our future – the past is gone and cannot be changed. The fact is, the people we have hurt will either accept us back in their lives, or they won't. Beating ourselves up for years will never change that outcome. But by forgiving ourselves, we *will* gain the peace we are seeking.

The other person we may not have thought to forgive is the Lord Himself. We may harbor old feelings of anger towards God because we believe that He wasn't there for us while we were going through our misery or abuse. Many people ask the question "If God loves me and He is supposed to be in control, why did He allow me to go through that pain?" The truth is that God allows people free will. He does not *intend* for us to suffer, but mankind brought sin into the world by their rebellion. As such, human experiences include pain and disappointment.

But personally, I wouldn't trade the pain and suffering I've endured for anything, because it's helped me to be sensitive to others going through terrible hardships. The beautiful part is that in the end, God *does* promise to bring good out of the evil that was intended for us, *if* we allow Him into our lives (Genesis 50:20).

- Is it possible you have not forgiven yourself? Have you forgiven God?

<u>Forgiveness pays great dividends!</u>
When we choose to forgive, we will be much more open to God's voice. We'll be free to hear Him reveal what He wants to do in our lives. As we learn to hear His Spirit's voice, He promises to order our steps, take our burdens, and show us where we need to grow, all the while giving us the strength to succeed (Proverbs 3:5-6; Matthew 11:28-30 and Ephesians 3:14-21). A loving, intimate relationship with God will change our empty lives into a life of spiritual, mental, emotional, and physical satisfaction and purpose. Only *He* can offer us the gifts of tremendous joy and peace.

Another reward we receive when we forgive is the freedom from replaying and reacting to those old negative 'tapes' that run through our heads. Forgiveness takes the power out of that old pain. The Lord says that "if we delight ourselves in Him, He will give us the desires of our hearts" (Psalm 37:3-5). The word 'delighting' in this scripture means thinking of Jesus as often as we would a lover. It includes talking to Him regularly, asking His opinion, seeking His direction, looking for His help in every area of our lives, and looking for ways to praise Him throughout the day. This lifestyle is not fully possible when we live with resentment and bitterness.

As we begin to let go of the past, we will have more time and energy to invest in this intimate relationship with our magnificent God. We will find that our hearts will begin to soften, and we'll desire the things He wants for us. It will be much easier to carry out His will. We'll also find that as we obey and trust Him, we will feel more secure in our lives, knowing that we are on the right road - *the one that was meant for us.* It's a beautiful process!

Finally, committing ourselves to God's ways and His timing will help us to worry less about what is ahead of us in our lives. As we come to know the Savior more fully, we'll find that we won't be so afraid of the future, because we'll understand that He is *absolutely* in control. When we come to believe that He is fighting for us, defending us, empowering us, loving us, and comforting us, we will be able to turn our focus away from ourselves and towards God and others.

<u>God will never leave us or forsake us</u>

He will be there for us no matter what - even if the worst should happen. He is the Only One who has the **power, the will, and the desire** to provide our every need throughout our lives. He knows our needs before we even ask. Believe it or not, *He set a path for our lives even before He created the earth* (Ephesians 1:4). And if we stay in relationship with Him until the end, we will have heaven to look forward to!

God fully desires for us to walk in His ways, because He knows that His path is the only one that will bring us deep, lasting joy and security. When we come to a place where we know His voice and hear His heartbeat; when we have received deep healing, and when we have had our greatest needs filled by the One Who made us, then we can begin to love ourselves and others fully. We will finally have the direction we need in life. We will gain a new confidence that we could never have received from the world, other people, or from our own efforts.

It is time to ask God to give you the desire to forgive those in your past. As God changes your heart and your ability to forgive, let those negative feelings go. Remember, it is essential to begin to pray for those people who have done you wrong, after you have spent time grieving your past situation with them. And be patient - it takes time and effort for our minds to think new thoughts. However, the rewards are awesome! You really can be free from the bondage of unforgiveness!

REFLECTION

It's important not to answer these questions quickly. Many times, we have buried these thoughts and feelings from our past just to help us cope. You may have to let God uncover some hidden feelings.

1. Are you experiencing any negative results from unforgiveness in your life?

2. Before you read this study, were you aware that God required you to forgive others?

3. List 3 fears you might have that keep you from forgiving others. Some fears might include:

"They will never forgive me in return"

"They will continue to hurt me if I forgive them"

"If I forgive them, then I am saying that what they did was okay"

4. What are some of the obstacles in your own life that may keep you from forgiving others? (some of these can include: pride, hardness of heart, fear, or denial of your own sinfulness)

5. Do you have problems forgiving yourself or God?

6. Just asking God to reveal your attitudes of unforgiveness will help you begin the road to freedom. If you are aware of a certain person you have not forgiven, ask for God's grace to overwhelm your heart so that you can release these feelings and forgive them.

7. If you feel it's impossible for you to forgive, ask God to give you the desire and ability to do this. Your plan might include: Each day this week, I will ask God to begin softening my heart. Then, each day next week, I will ask Him to begin revealing those people in my life whom I need to forgive. And the next week, I will start praying for them. Writing your experiences down will really help you to keep track of your growth. What seems impossible now will become a reality later on. Try it!

NOTES

FREEDOM

*Jesus Christ **IS** Our Freedom!*

What is the first thing you think of when you hear the word 'free'? Maybe you feel skeptical when you hear someone say 'It's free'. Most of us have learned from experience that few things are ever truly free in life. And more importantly, many of us have habits or traits that make us feel like we are in bondage. Often, we wonder if there is a chance that we can really be free.

<u>Jesus and our freedom</u>

Did you know that as human beings, we are *born* into sin (Psalm 14:1-3 and Romans 3:9-12)? Many believe that we are 'basically good people'. But the Bible says that our hearts are *deceitfully wicked* (Jeremiah 17:9-10)! We are enslaved to our sin nature (Romans 7:14-25). And there is not a thing we can do to relieve our sinful condition without God's intervention.

The Greek meaning for the word 'free' means 'to liberate; to cease being a slave; and to be exempt from liability'. From God's point of view, we are definitely liable for our sin. But Jesus came for the very purpose of setting us free from this inborn disposition (1 Corinthians 1:30; 1 John 3:4-6; and Revelation 1:5). He knew we would never be able to overcome our sin nature on our own, no matter how hard we tried.

Why did Jesus have to die for my sin?

Jesus is called our Savior, which implies that we needed to be saved *from* something. He *chose to come to us,* because He loved us before the world was created (1 John 4:9-10). He wanted to set us free from our sin nature, so that we could be reconciled to God and enjoy an intimate relationship with Him (2 Corinthians 5:18-21). He paid the penalty that God demanded for our sin. We couldn't use our own lives for payment, because we are not holy enough; our life would have been a filthy sacrifice. Since God is perfect and we are not, the sacrifice He required was a pure and spotless payment, a payment with NO sin attached (Exodus 12:5 and 1 Peter 1:18-19).

Jesus, fully human and fully God, was the only person alive who never sinned (Hebrews 4:14-16; and 1 Peter 2:22-25). So He was the only perfect One who could accomplish this feat. *Someone* needed to make the payment for our sin, so that we who are unholy could come near to God in His holiness. That price included death – shed blood as payment for sin. God's Word says that only someone's life can pay for a life, so without the shedding of blood, there is no remission (freedom, pardon, forgiveness, or deliverance) of sin (Leviticus 17:11 and Hebrews 9:22).

I'm free!

It's easy to sin! We have always been 'free' to disobey, but real strength and character are proven in our ability to stand against the fleshly desires we have. Without Jesus, we are slaves to our sin, completely unable to choose godliness and righteousness. This is because the Holy Spirit is unable to live in our old, sinful flesh. But as we commit our lives to God, the Spirit will work in us to transform us into Christ's likeness (2 Corinthians 3:16-18). Then, we will be able to make positive choices that honor God, because *He* will give us the supernatural strength to do what He wants us to do (Philippians 2:13).

Jesus redeems us by His blood, which blots out our sin so that we can be intimate with Him (Isaiah 1:18 and 1 John 1:9). When Christ reconciled, or brought us back to God, He gave our spirits life (John 3:5-8 and Ephesians 2:4-7), and the Holy Spirit now lives inside every genuine believer (Romans 8:9). That's amazing!

Because of Jesus' sacrifice, we are now truly free from the curse of the law, from our selfishness, and from the influence of the devil and the world (Romans 3:21-26 and Romans 6:1-18). The power of the Cross gives us new life, because the very power that raised Jesus from the dead is available to us to overcome our sin nature – our 'flesh' (Colossians 1:19-22 and Galatians 6:14-16).

The Bible says that we are created *anew* in Christ Jesus (Ephesians 2:10). This means we have been created **twice** – once when we are naturally born, and again when we are spiritually born. And because of God's wonderful provision, our rebirth results in the Holy Spirit being able to bring forth His *eternal* fruit in our lives. This particular kind of fruit draws people to Jesus, and as such, Christians are able to help reconcile other lost souls to God. Bringing others to Christ is a harvest that will last forever, and it's what we will be rewarded for when we get to heaven.

If I'm free in Jesus, do I still have to adhere to God's Old Testament laws?

In the Old Testament, God's 'law' included the Ten Commandments, plus the moral and civil requirements that were given to the Hebrew people in order for them to succeed as a nation, and more importantly, as God's own people (Deuteronomy 7:6). God's purpose for forming the Israelite nation was to exhibit His love through them to the known world. Today, when we hear the phrase 'the law', it usually refers to the Ten Commandments. Many of the old ceremonial and civil laws are no longer in effect, because they don't apply to our culture anymore. However, God's *moral* laws are eternal and they are relevant for every culture, every season, and every generation.

When Jesus came, He was the perfect fulfillment of God's moral law (Colossians 1:15-20). Therefore, He summed up the Old Testament law into two statements: "Love the Lord your God with all your heart, all your soul, and all your mind, and love your neighbor as yourself" (Deuteronomy 6:4-9 and Matthew 22:36-40). Simply put, when we love God with our whole being, He gives us the capacity to love others beyond our own ability. And when we love the Lord and others, we 'fulfill' the requirements of the law, because we no longer want to cause harm to God, others, or ourselves.

To further understand this concept, let's look back to Jesus' day. The Jewish society he had entered was rampant with religious leaders who had developed <u>hundreds</u> of extra laws that were beyond what God had originally ordained. These man-made rules dictated everything from the way the people were to behave during times of worship, what they ate, how they spoke, how they were to dress, and how they were to conduct business.

The problem with most of these extra laws was 1. They were not God's requirements, but were an attempt to force the people into subjection; 2. They had become so oppressed by their own rules, they had lost the joy of the Lord and of serving others; and 3. Because of their pride and greed, their hearts were completely hardened to the Lord (Isaiah 29:13). To them, it was all about the 'rule-keeping'. Not only that, but they had become VERY proud of their laws, and liked to strut around town acting 'holy'. They robbed from the poor and demanded respect from the common people, but they themselves did not live godly lives. This is what Jesus was so upset about when He confronted them (Matthew 12:33-37 and 23:27-28).

Now, before we look down on these people for their attitudes, we have to remember that we as Christians can get caught up in exactly the same cycle. We impose our little rules upon others, and then feel superior because of our self-made regulations! Certainly, we have all had the experience of being around people who act like they are super-spiritual. They are proud and they like others to think they know it all, but they lack love, joy, peace and compassion. And they're a real nightmare to be around!

Ironically, we may even feel inferior to them because they 'seem' to have it together in the 'religious' department. However, people who follow 'Christian rules' with no joy or love in their lives are fueled by motives that **STINK** to the Lord. Far from 'pleasing' God, they shame Him (Luke 18:9-14). Since Jesus came to save the lost and empower the downtrodden, using this kind of proud and calloused behavior with unbelievers and weaker Christians is a slap in the Lord's face.

<u>The big payback</u>

It is human nature to repay someone when we have been given something, and it's no different when we desire to 'pay' Jesus back for the price He paid for us. The problem with this mindset is that it really gets in the way when it comes to our salvation. We feel the need to DO something to be saved. Or, we work harder and harder so Jesus will love us more. "Maybe if I go to church more, or give more money, or say more hail Mary's , or 'try' to be nicer to people, *then* I will have more brownie points with God", we say. Even the most genuine Christian struggles with this concept. As born-again Christians, we may still feel the need to pay the debt for our sin. If you have any of the following feelings, you may still be chained to your old thinking:

You feel constant guilt about your past sin even after you have asked Jesus for forgiveness

You are always measuring yourself and find yourself coming up less than perfect

Or, you are so ashamed of yourself that you have trouble facing God, then you need to understand the GRACE that He has applied to your life because of His absolute love for you. *Jesus has already paid the price for your sin and my sin, both now and forever.* Trying to pay Jesus back would be like receiving a gift of a brand new car. Several days after you get the car, you return to the dealer and ask if you can make expensive and burdensome monthly payments on your already-paid-for car! That sounds ludicrous, but at times, that is exactly what we do with God! We want to go back and pay for a transaction that is already finished.

So instead of spending our time and energy trying to earn God's love, favor, and provision, we need to **refocus** our efforts. We need to get away from trying to earn His attention and affection, because it's already there! While we *are* required to do something in our walk with Jesus, it is *not* working to cover up our sin, making ourselves look better, or making others think that we don't have problems. What Jesus really wants in return for His magnificent gift is our obedience that results from a heart full of love and devotion.

Our job is to cling to Christ,
to get to know Him better,
to fall in love with Him through prayer
to diligently search the Bible for His Truth,
to fully serve Him by giving of our time, talents, and treasure to others,
and to spend time with genuine Christians who will influence our lives for good.

- Do you feel that you need to 'do more' in order for God to love you?

Uncommitted 'Christians'

A frequent question from unbelievers is this: "If Jesus is real and He came to set people free, why do so many Christians act just like those who *don't* follow Jesus"? While we all make mistakes, there are people whose *lifestyles* fail to reflect the principles that God has given us in scripture. These people lack a deep commitment to Christ, because they have not yet made the decision to 'die to their flesh' (Colossians 3:5-9 and Galatians 5:24-25). Dying to our flesh involves making choices that actively, willfully place our own desires, dreams, goals, attitudes, and sins in the hands of God. It means choosing to spend quality time in prayer, and committing ourselves to reading and obeying the Bible regularly. And it entails making a conscious effort to live out God's will with His Spirit's power.

We can see a striking example of crucifying the flesh when we observe the underground Christians in many nations around the world that prohibit Christianity. These are powerful groups of people who are willing to risk their very lives in order to spread the good news of Christ. Their focus is sharp and unswerving; they know the exact cost of their faith and they don't mess around! There is no 'maybe I'll act like a Christian today, maybe I won't tomorrow' attitude. They LIVE the life that is laid out in scripture. They *constantly* die to their flesh. Because they are putting their lives on the line, there ***is*** no middle ground for them. This is what many American Christians are missing. We are so busy being part of the world that the world cannot tell the Christians apart from themselves.

This is where many unbelievers justifiably have trouble with Christianity. They see there is no power in what Christians say or do. The truth is, we have been **bought with a price (**1Corinthians 6:19-20) by God's own death. If you say you are a Christian and bear no fruit or glory for His kingdom in your life, then you need to do some serious soul-searching. God saved us so that we could glorify Him by bringing lost souls into the kingdom (Romans 1:5). The Christian life is full of spiritual blessing, but there is also a requirement of repentance and obedience. We cannot enjoy God's blessings without sacrificing our own time, talent, and money for His purposes.

Make no mistake - some will find themselves face-to-face with Jesus on Judgment Day, believing they are going to heaven forever. But they will be horrified to hear Jesus say "Depart from Me, I never knew you" (Matthew 7:15-23 and Matthew 25:1-13). We dishonor His name when we call ourselves Christians and yet act nothing like Him. We cheapen His sacrifice and His grace when we continue to live selfish and sinful lives. What a grievance to our Lord, who paid the price so that we COULD be different!

Christian freedom - it's a heart thing

We have already learned that Christian freedom is not about rules and regulations. If we are trying to overcome sin by willpower or 'brainpower', we will run into real trouble. The Christian life will end up like a death sentence, instead of the thrill that it really is. The real secret to overcoming our sin is to diligently seek Jesus. We please Him when we delight ourselves in Him. As He changes us, we begin to see our sin as it really is, because we are being cleansed by His presence. We then come to a place where we WANT to obey Him, *because we fall in love with Him*. Instead of demanding "What have you done for ME lately", our faces should be turned towards God, asking Him "What can I do for you, my Lord?"

The only way we can return Jesus' awesome gift is to live a life fully encompassed by Him.

God's Word gives implicit instructions about what we are to do and how we are supposed to behave in our Christian walk. And we all know that love empowers us to do things beyond our own strength, and outside of our own selfishness. When we obey the Lord out of *love*, then we begin to understand that His requirements for us are because He loves us, not because He's trying to boss us around and keep us from having fun.

It's the same analogy as with our children. Do we set parameters around our kids because we are mean and we're trying to stifle them? No! It's because we love them and want them to mature into the best people that they have the potential to become. And if our children disobey, there are consequences for them. We know from our own experience that if they continue to disregard our rules, they may get hurt. And the intimacy of the relationship is lost with their rebellion. It's exactly the same thing with us, as God's children.

I know that before I gave my life to Jesus, I *thought* I was free because I did whatever I wanted. But as I look back, I realize I never was really free when I lived by the world's morals and values. Instead of enjoying my choices, I felt afraid and guilty. I knew my life had no purpose - it was a total waste. I was lonely and I hated myself. But when I started making choices to honor God and let His Spirit fill me, I felt genuine freedom for the first time in my life. I now had *God's* power that allowed me to **choose** to do good, and to make right choices. Besides that, I had <u>never</u> experienced unconditional love until I met Jesus, and just being in this love relationship gave me supernatural strength and confidence (Titus 3:3-8). I came to understand that there was a purpose for my life, and God was going to use me for His glory. In time, the Holy Spirit gave me His gifts of love, joy, peace, and hope. And I have never regretted my decision. ☺

- Do you feel free right now, or are the cares of this world weighing you down?
- Do you believe you can be free?
- Are you having trouble making decisions that support your faith?

- Are you afraid to let God change your life because you are comfortable right where you are?

Don't scare them away!

Many people have never felt unconditional love, and this is what draws them into the arms of our Savior. The unsaved may have the misconception that they have to 'clean up' before they can enter a church or get near God. This misconstrued belief is reinforced oftentimes when they are hammered by Christians about what they need to 'do' to gain favor with God. If we insist that they begin conforming immediately to our uptight regulations, we will end up turning them away from our Wonderful Jesus! Jesus came to set us free, not to further enslave us (Acts 15:10-11).

The reality is, people know that they sin. Somewhere inside, they know they are guilty. So the last thing they need to hear when they come to church is how 'bad' they are and how much they need to change to become like 'us'! They need to hear about the love and grace of Jesus. Peter calls it 'the milk of the Word' (1 Peter 2:2-3), because new believers are just that – babies in the faith. Obviously, this does not mean that they are not required to mature in the faith, or that they will be allowed to continually bask in their sin, refusing to let God change their lives. True conversion shows a changed life. But they will find out soon enough what sacrifice is necessary for the privilege of serving King Jesus. And if they need help rejecting their old life, God will deal with them *through us, as we administer genuine, loving discipline* the way Jesus did .

- What are you doing right now in your life in order to draw the lost to Jesus? Name two things you can start doing today.

So, how can I ensure that I *stay* free in Christ?

It doesn't take long as a Christian to hear sayings like 'living in the power of the Holy Spirit', or 'using the Spirit's power to live a holy life', or 'a Spirit-filled Christian life'. God sent the Holy Spirit to give us power to overcome our flesh and this world. If we fail to live by the Holy Spirit's power, we will eventually feel that our 'carnal' liberty is being restricted. This means that our flesh will start to want to take over again, and what used to attract us in the world will once again entice us. And the chances are, we will be drawn back to our old life. Trying to be obedient to the Lord at this point will feel like a noose around our neck. I have seen this happen many times. Someone comes to the faith out of a life of drugs, gangs, abuse, or strict religion. They are so happy to find Jesus! But after a few months of 'trying' to be a Christian, they lose their resolve and go right back to the life they came from.

But when we live by the Spirit, He supernaturally imparts to our minds that our salvation is complete. He gives us power to live the way God wants us to live. By His power, we understand that everything God has designed for us is for our very best. The way to receive the Holy Spirit is to 'repent, be baptized, and then you will receive the gift of the Holy Spirit' (Acts 2:38). The gift of repentance and salvation is not cheap, and God's power in our lives cannot be faked. But when you start to experience godly desires, thoughts, and deeds, you'll realize that He is empowering you, and that there is no greater life than to lay it down at the Master's feet.

Suppose you're in a place where you feel that Christianity 'just didn't work' for you. Maybe you have been dabbling in your old life, trying to get relief from things you know have never brought you happiness. Maybe you are obsessing on your children, finances, or your relationship. Perhaps, you feel you have worked really hard at this 'Christianity business', but have really made no progress. Or maybe you feel disenchanted by the promises God gave you through the Bible, such as "He promised to set me free, and I'm more miserable than ever".

If this sounds like what you are going through, realize that this is the very time when you need intercessory prayer and counsel from a pastor or trusted Christian friend. It is essential to dig into the Word and spend time in personal, private prayer to fortify your soul. Remember, our salvation is sure, if we are genuinely born again. But if there comes a point where we completely reject Jesus, we have to wonder how sincere our 'conversion' was (Hebrews 3:5-14 and Hebrews 6:4-6).

True conversion produces long standing commitment and fruit. And while we certainly will go through hills and valleys in our walk, the truth is that in every decision we make, we are either moving toward Jesus or towards the enemy. This is why Jesus said "Either you believe in Me and serve Me, or you are serving the enemy" (Matthew 12:30), *paraphrase mine*. Satan will try to reclaim you, but it is your choice whether or not he will succeed.

So before you run back to your old life, realize that genuine freedom is NOT rejecting God's ways– that is *recklessness!* Genuine Christian liberty is the choice to stay <u>within</u> His boundaries. Contrary to our society's attitude on freedom – "I'm free to do whatever I want no matter who is affected", true Christian freedom is full of self-control and a resulting concern for the welfare of others. The exhilarating byproduct of choosing to follow Jesus Christ is experiencing a profound love that comes from a pure heart, a clear conscience, and a genuine faith (1Timothy 1:5). And we also receive the gifts of the Holy Spirit (Galatians 5:22-23).

- At this point in your life: Are you a) very involved with Jesus , b) sort of living on the fence of Christianity and the world, or c) making choices that exclude Jesus from your life?

<u>It isn't easy</u>

It would be a lie to say that living the Christian life is easy. But how easy was your life without Jesus? Life is oftentimes a struggle no matter what. We have all found that relationships take work. We know that any worthwhile project takes determination, strength, and energy. And anytime we want to abstain from overindulgence, it's usually not very fun.

It's no different in our relationship with God. This relationship is the most important one we will ever choose to enter into, and it takes time, effort, and sacrifice. But when we authentically accept Jesus into our hearts, and we receive the immeasurable gift of eternal salvation, there is a reason to be exceedingly joyous, because we have been declared 'not guilty' by the blood of Jesus Christ. We have literally been set free.

If we stay the course with Jesus, we will soon find that He is there for our every need. His Spirit is the only One that can produce godly fruit in us, if we allow Him. If we are persistent in our faith, we will find that Jesus gives us so much more than anything we could receive from this world (Colossians 1:23). The bottom line is that we can choose to submit to God's will and His timing in order to receive genuine freedom, or we can give up and take the path of least resistance, and go back to our old lives (Galatians 6:7-10). Just remember, God always wants to lead you back into the 'path of everlasting life'. And we receive true freedom by living in submission to the path that God has ordained for our lives through the power of the Holy Spirit.

REFLECTION

1. What does Christian freedom mean?

2. What price was paid so we could be free?

3. What are 3 things I can do to begin getting closer to the Lord?

4. Am I afraid to let the Holy Spirit make a difference in my life? Why?

5. Does my life draw people to the Lord? Can someone tell that I am a Christian by the way I talk and behave?

6. Do I believe that if I'm a 'good enough' person, I will tip the scale just enough to get to heaven? Think about this carefully – our 'Christian' response may be "No, Jesus paid the price for me". But we all struggle with the idea that we can make brownie points when we are being 'good'.

NOTES

GUILT

*God's love for us is **far more powerful** than our sin and our guilt.*

Does guilt play a major role in your life? Maybe you feel guilty about not raising your children right. Or you may carry guilt over a failed marriage. Perhaps there is something you did as a child that you continue to harbor guilty feelings about. In reality, most of us have had trouble with guilt at some point in our lives. And some of us are even *consumed* by our guilt.

What IS guilt?

The word guilt is defined as "The responsibility for committing an offense that carries a legal penalty, as determined by a court or other legal authority". I call this the 'action' part of guilt. When we do something wrong, we pay a price. This can be a spiritual, financial, emotional, physical, or psychological penalty.

It is also "An awareness of having done something wrong, accompanied by feelings of shame and regret". I call this the 'feeling' part of guilt. Feeling remorse about our actions is like a warning light, letting us know when we are doing something contrary to God's will (Romans 3:23) . The Lord actually designed healthy guilt to keep us on the right track.

But I didn't know!

The only way a healthy society functions is to have legal and moral boundaries. Soon after mankind was created, God began forming the Hebrew nation. He chose a special nation so that the world could see His power and glory through His people's faith and behavior. He wanted to be their God and to embrace them as His very own treasure (Deuteronomy 7:6-11).

As a new nation, God needed to outline civil, moral, and ceremonial laws that included penalties for misbehavior in order for them to be able to live in harmony. These regulations weren't to keep them from having fun; on the contrary, it was so they could avoid conflict and chaos. God promised that if they obeyed His will, they would be able to live in peace and prosperity (Exodus 6:7 and Leviticus 26:12). And His principles have not changed since then. Many people we see today are miserable, because they are choosing to live in ways that oppose God's design for them.

In addition, God's commandments were given because people needed to know what was right and wrong, and what He expected of them (Romans 5:12-13). Once these directives were in place, the people could no longer feign innocence when they disobeyed (Romans 3:19-20). In today's terms, for example, we can't honestly say "Oh officer, I didn't know I was supposed to stop at that stop sign", because we know what the stop sign means. And as much as we may dislike the regulations we are forced to follow, we know that if there were no rules, we would live in complete confusion and disorder.

We also know the penalties for disobeying the law. We understand that we will pay the price of time, money, and/or energy to make up for our rebellion. But there is a much more severe penalty for living our lives contrary to God's ways than just getting a ticket or going to jail. Even though we may not reap the consequences of our sin immediately, we are sure to suffer down the road for our poor choices. We can either ignore God's ways now, and pay the price then, or we can receive God's solution to the dilemma of sin in our lives now (Romans 3:21-28).

While we are perfectly able to make the right choice about something as simple as a stop sign, we are absolutely incapable of living a life of holiness for God apart from a relationship with Jesus Christ and His Holy Spirit. Our sin nature keeps us from consistently making wise choices (Romans, Chapter 7). In the spiritual realm, the Bible **is** our 'stop sign'. It tells us when we are veering away from the life that God wants us to live (Hebrews 4:12-13 and 2 Timothy 3:16-17).

God wants to be *our* God, too, and embrace us as His own people (Ephesians 1:12-14; Ephesians 2:14-16; Titus 2:11-14, and 1 Peter 2:9-10). And the only way this can happen is if we are in an *active* relationship with Him. Believing in Jesus and making Him the Master of our lives is the most important choice we will *ever* make in this life.

I'm guilty!

The truth is, as human beings, we are guilty, just by being alive! We are naturally contrary to God, because we are born into sin and instinctively make choices that are not in alignment with His will (Romans 3:9-12 and 8:5-8). Indeed, we hardly finish the second chapter of the first book of the Bible before we witness the original sin and guilt that began with Adam and Eve. Genesis 2:25 says that they felt no shame when they were naked in the garden together. But right after this in Genesis 3:7, God tells us that they felt shame. How could this have happened so quickly?

Let's find out in Genesis 2:25 - 3:21:

The devil speaks to Eve	Genesis 3:1
Eve quotes the Word of God	3:2
Satan lies to Eve	3:4-5

Eve **believes the devil instead of the Word of God**	3:6a
Eve quickly encourages her husband to share in her sin	3:6b
Their disobedience cuts them off from intimacy with God and each other	3:7
Adam refuses to take responsibility for his actions, and blames Eve and God	3:12
Eve blames satan, the serpent (the devil made me do it!)	3:13b
God lovingly makes provision for their sin by shedding innocent blood to cover their sin and guilt (the animal had to have been slain in order for Adam and Eve to receive the skins for clothing)	3:20-21

So we see that SIN is what brought **guilt** into the picture. Shame overtook Adam and Eve in a short time because of their *choice* to disobey what God had spoken to them. Immediately, their relationship with their beloved Lord changed, and they no longer felt completely at ease with Him. They also began disagreeing with each other! It is amazing that this sequence of events has been the blueprint for mankind ever since. We disbelieve and disobey God. Then, we try to justify ourselves. We blame others, and then try to get them to share in our misery. And sadly, the ultimate result of sin, as well as guilt, is separation from God.

- Can you relate any of the above attitudes to your own life?

<u>Sin is as old as the hills</u>

We know that sin has been around since the very first human beings, but it's interesting to know that God quickly designed a way for their sin and guilt to be covered. In the book of Leviticus, the Lord instructed the Israelites to sacrifice two goats to purify the people, so that their sin could be dealt with. One goat was designated for the forgiveness of their sins, and the other goat was symbolic for removing the guilt associated with their sin. This goat was aptly called the 'scapegoat' (Leviticus 16:6-10).The reason why a blood sacrifice from an animal was required is because there is *life* in the blood of a living being (Leviticus 17:11). A life had to be traded for a life, because 'without the shedding of blood, there is no forgiveness of sins' (Hebrews 9:22). It was also a 'word picture' to show them that their sin was associated with death and required a very heavy price.

God even determined different categories for their guilt, called 'guilt offerings' (Leviticus 5:14-19). The first guilt offering we see was for those that 'sinned against the holy things of the Lord'. This offering dealt with intentional sin, but it also covered acts of forgetfulness or lack of attention. The second category covered someone if they weren't sure if they were guilty or not. It was available for the person with the guilty conscience, and it was an opportunity for them to ask and receive God's assurance of forgiveness. And the third offense requiring a guilt offering was for the person who pleaded innocence, but was actually guilty. They were expected to pay everything back to the offended party, and pay interest, too.

The Hebrew people were required to make daily and yearly sacrifices for their sin down through the centuries. But when Jesus came, He paid the debt once and for all (Hebrews 9:11-14 and 9:18-22). He *was* the unblemished, Spotless Lamb that was called for in the Old Testament (Exodus 12:5 and 1 Peter 1:18-19). That is why He is called "The Lamb of God" (John 1:29-30). This complex sacrificial system was used to point God's people (Israel) towards the Messiah that would eventually come. It was instituted so that when Jesus arrived, the people would already be familiar with the concept of the shedding of blood for their sins. Unfortunately, most of these people were so entrenched in their 'religious' ways, they didn't recognize Jesus when

He came to save them. But that was precisely why He **chose** to die – so He could pay the price so we could have reconciliation with God (Colossians 1:15-22).

Why is Jesus so important?

There are many religions that refer to themselves as 'Christians'. However, the way to tell if they are authentic believers or not, is what they believe about Jesus. Many think that He was just a 'good man', or a 'prophet'. But the Bible says that Jesus Christ is the second Person of the Godhead Trinity, and as such, He is also the Eternal God (Isaiah 9:6-7, John 1:1-5 and John 17:20-21). The 'Word' referred to in this scripture in John is Jesus Christ, the *Living* Word. We also call the Bible the 'Written Word', which is also ***alive*** and powerful (Hebrews 4:12). So you see, the Word (Jesus) and the Word (the Bible), are both living, dynamic powers that are capable of transforming our lives!

Most of us have heard the quote "In the name of the Father, the Son, and the Holy Spirit". We may not really think about it, but the implication is extremely important. In the culture that the Bible was written, it would have been sacrilege to put these names together in the same sentence if they did not have equal standing. Nothing in their minds was comparable to God Almighty. As a matter of fact, the Jews didn't even *say* the word 'God', because they had so much reverence for Him.

The Bible makes it clear that God the Father, God the Son (Jesus), and God the Holy Spirit have been together for eternity past, even as the earth was being formed (Genesis 1:26). The Hebrew word for 'God' in this scripture is 'Elohim', which translates as **pleural** for God. This does not mean there are three Gods, as some people think. Christianity is a 'monotheistic' faith. Mono' means 'one' and theistic comes from the word 'Theo', which means 'God'. The fact is, the Father, Son, and Holy Spirit are all equal in power, majesty, and authority, but they have different functions. It's the same concept as our government. There are the Executive, Legislative, and Judicial parts.

And they are all considered 'The Government'. They have equal power, but they all perform different roles.

It is essential to understand and believe that Jesus is God, because only GOD could have made the sacrifice that was necessary to pardon our sin-debt. Think of it this way: If another person died to try to make up for your sin, that would be a powerful act. However, their sacrifice wouldn't be able to make you right with God, because the other person is a sinner, too. But because Jesus (as God) was the only perfect human being, He alone was uniquely qualified and faultless enough to be able to bring genuine holiness to our lives, so that the darkness of our sin could be blotted out (Isaiah 53). He 'bought' us with His own precious blood, and this very act gives Him the right to demand our total allegiance and affection (1 Peter 1:17-19).

Incidentally, Isaiah 53 was written about Jesus nearly **700** years before He came to this earth. It was prophesied far in advance, so that we would recognize Jesus as the miraculous answer to God's plan. Jesus is the reason why we don't have to shed the blood of animals any longer. Colossians 2:13-15 says that as we come to God in genuine repentance, we receive forgiveness and that our debts are canceled. When Jesus forgives our sins, the transaction is finished (1 John 1:9). As a matter of fact, He literally *forgets* them (Jeremiah 31:33-34)!

- Do you believe that when you genuinely ask for forgiveness, that God truly releases you from your sin and forgets your misdeeds?

<u>Jesus came so we could be free</u>

It is essential to keep our eyes on Jesus and remember what His mission was when He came to save us.

JESUS DIED FOR US to:

Purify us,
to bring us close to Him,
to forgive us,
to set us *free,*
to heal us,
to empower us to live for Him
and to bring us home to heaven to live with Him forever!

Even though we are born at war with God, Jesus Christ has reversed our isolation from the Father by His death and resurrection. By accepting the sacrifice that Jesus made to satisfy God's anger towards sin (1John 2:1-2), *we* now become holy and blameless because of *Jesus*' purity (Col 1:21-23a). This is what it means when the Bible says that we are 'in Christ' (Ephesians 2:10).

If we have allowed Jesus to come into our hearts, and sorrowfully asked Him for forgiveness, we need to **accept** that it is done. To relive our sins and continue to beat ourselves up is like having a judge release you from the courtroom a free person, and then returning to beg him to put you in jail! Since God Himself cleanses, forgives, and forgets our sin, we are basically saying that He did not do enough to redeem us, if we continue to hold onto our guilt. We are ignoring His sacrifice. And since the Bible is God's Truth to us, we are calling Him a liar when we refuse to believe that we are forgiven.

- Can you think of a couple of areas where you have asked God to forgive you, but you still hold onto your grief and guilt?

Two kinds of guilt

There are two kinds of guilt – healthy and unhealthy. We have seen that 'healthy guilt' is one way that God lets us know we are doing something wrong. It is what brings us to repentance (2 Corinthians 7:10a). Genuine repentance means not only turning *from* our ways, but turning *towards* the Lord's ways. Healthy guilt focuses on changing our ways so we begin to please God. It includes feeling sorrow about being separated from Him, and taking whatever steps we need to in order to restore our relationship with Him. If we feel guilty because we are continuing to sin, that is good! Hopefully, this will make us uncomfortable enough to cause us to turn from our unholy behavior.

However, one of the dangers of **living** in this state of guilt without changing is that we start to feel uneasy about coming to the Lord in prayer. We may think that He is so disgusted with us, He doesn't even want to hear from us. We also may feel awkward about coming to church, because we feel like hypocrites. But this is the *very* time that God does not want us to stay away! We need to receive healing from the Lord, and forgiveness for our sins! We must hear the Word of God preached, and we need the strength and support of other believers who are struggling in their Christian walk, as well.

It's essential that we see the lives of other people being restored because they are choosing to leave their sin. This gives us hope that we can also overcome our own weaknesses. When we isolate ourselves, we stop seeing things from God's point of view, and we digress further into our sin. This is exactly where the enemy wants us – in the dark, alone, afraid, and full of guilt and shame. Once we're there, it becomes even more difficult to move forward. We lose hope for the future and in our ability to change. And we are of no value to God's kingdom when we live like this.

Unhealthy guilt

Unhealthy guilt focuses on *ourselves.* It is described in Second Corinthians 7:10b as 'worldly sorrow'. This is the kind of guilt that produces no motivation for repentance or change. This is when we're 'sorry' because we got caught, or because someone is mad at us for hurting them. But there is no remorse for the actual sin. Unhealthy guilt enslaves us to our past, and no good can come from it. This type of 'guilt' can result in spiritual death, because it ultimately alienates us from God.

How do I know what kind of guilt I'm feeling?

The way to determine if our guilt is healthy or not is to examine our behavior. Does our guilt move us towards God, and away from our sin? Or are we becoming more self-absorbed, continuing to think of ways to justify our behavior, and feeling less desire for the things of God?

Some ways that guilt can manifest are:
fear of change,
inability to have close relationships,
fear of intimacy,
fear of commitment,
or, an inability to step out of your comfort zone.

You may experience:
weight gain or loss,
become self-destructive,
blame yourself in every situation,
be unable to forgive yourself,
develop physical pain,

isolate,
be terrified to feel your deep emotions,
be unable to cry or grieve,
and in serious situations, become suicidal.

- If you live with unresolved feelings of guilt, write down how many of these symptoms have you experienced in your life. (Obviously, there are a range of reasons we might experience these problems, but just consider the possibility that guilt may be a link).

But I don't *feel* guilty....

Then, of course, are the times when we *are* guilty, but we may not *feel* guilty. So we need to be aware that just because we don't *feel* guilty about something doesn't mean we are *not* guilty! Ephesians 4:17-24 says our conscience can be "seared", which is like putting meat on a hot grill. Over time, unconfessed and unrepented sin can 'burn' our conscience and our emotions, so that we feel less and less healthy guilt. And the longer we go against what we know is right, the more our emotions are hardened.

This kind of behavior leads to repressed guilt, because our guilt is still there, regardless if we acknowledge it or not. When we shove our guilt aside so that we can continue doing what we want to do, but we know it's wrong, our guilt 'goes' somewhere! Even though we may not 'feel' sorry for our actions, our subconscious still has to deal with our rebellion somehow. Even the medical and psychological community realizes this phenomenon; it is well known that many of the physical, emotional, and mental ailments we see today are a direct result of guilt. *God knew that the guilt attached to our sin would be as devastating as the consequences of the sin itself.*

- If you struggle with (or have struggled with) guilt, did you experience healthy or unhealthy guilt?
- How did it make you feel? Did it lead you to repentance and changed behavior? Or did you continue to sin, experiencing more misery and guilt?

Forgiven, but not relieved

We may experience another type of unhealthy guilt. Perhaps we *are* truly sorry, and we have confessed our sin and changed our behavior. But we still hold onto the burdensome feelings of guilt and cannot let go of the pain associated with our sin. This can destroy us spiritually, physically, emotionally, and mentally. It is also a powerful tool that Satan uses to keep us in bondage.

We may even feel sorry for ourselves in this state, but we need to realize that it is our responsibility to get into the Word of God and let Him transform our minds. If we are still guilt-ridden after we have asked for forgiveness, then in reality, we are actually *choosing* to relive those old memories, and we are *choosing* to beat ourselves up over our past sin. If we continue with this thinking, we often end up with a 'victim' mentality. We may end up feeling like the world has hurt us and now 'owes us'. And even though we may despise feeling this way, the truth is that if we refuse to change our thinking to God's way of thinking, we are *making the choice* to dwell on our bad feelings. God wants our feelings and thoughts to come under the subjection of His Truth, so that we become stable in our thinking.

It may seem strange to realize that we may have become so accustomed to our guilt that we are reluctant to let it go. Maybe we believe at some level that we are giving up part of our identity. Quite possibly, we might even hold onto our guilt because it allows us to feel that we are *doing something to pay for our sin and failures.* We may feel the need to suffer, because we caused someone else harm, and we feel that our pain will somehow make up for what we have done. Or we might believe that if we let go of our guilt, then the 'bond' with the person we have hurt will be broken.

Philippians 3:13-14 says that we are to 'forget' the past. This does not mean that we stop remembering what we have gone through, or what we have done. Actually, keeping account of our past mistakes can have a positive effect on us by keeping us from going back to our old life. It's also beneficial to share our failures and victories with others, and use our past as a testimony of God's grace and provision in our lives. But Paul is talking about not *dwelling* on our past mistakes. Those deeds have already happened and the damage has been done. Our job is to *let go* of the negative *feelings* associated with those misdeeds. We need to make room in our minds for God to work. Don't forget that He is the Master at turning our bad choices around for **His** glory! (Genesis 50:20). Because our feelings can so easily deceive us, we must immerse ourselves in God's Word and train our minds to believe what *God* says about our sin and guilt.

- The Bible is the cleansing and comforting agent that the Holy Spirit uses to bring healing to your mind and emotions. Can you make a commitment to yourself and to God that you will begin reading His Word for at least 15 minutes every day? The book of John is a great place to start.

Hope is on the way!

Jesus came to this earth to bring us back into relationship with God. He came to save us, not to judge us (John 12:44-50). He proved His power over all spiritual forces by His own sacrificial death and resurrection. We now have the same power to overcome our sin, because we have the Holy Spirit living inside of us (Romans 8:11). And when Jesus forgives us, and gives us victory over our sin, we need to *decide* to part with the guilt that accompanies it. It is our *choice* whether we use the power available to us from the Holy Spirit to live a life of peace, joy, and hope. The Spirit of God can and will give us the power to let go of our guilt, if we only let Him.

Remember, we have always had the ability to sin! Before we were saved, we didn't have the *power* to make choices that honored God. However, we now have the freedom to live a righteous life. Jesus put that choice back in our hands when He triumphed over death and sin. We read in Isaiah 53:5-6 that He bore (took upon Himself) our sins *and* guilt. He erased them by His sacrifice. That is the mystery of the Cross and the Blood. Now we have *HIS* power, not merely our own.

<u>So, how can I be free of guilt?</u>

Praise be to God for giving us the solution through His Spirit and His Word! Psalm 32 speaks about confession and repentance. What is interesting is that the Hebrew word for 'guilt' in verse 2 is translated as 'sin' in the Greek; they are inseparable. The psalmist knew that the result of confession and repentance would be the overwhelming joy of a restored relationship with the Lord. Notice this scripture covers emotional, physical, mental and spiritual healing! After we are restored, we can be certain that God will protect us because we are living a life according to His will (verse 8). He purifies our hearts as we continue to turn towards Him, which allows us to hear Him more easily. And as we continue this healthy process, He gives us more power to obey Him the next time, which will allow us even more peace.

We need to *choose* to quit 'playing the old tapes' that tell us we have done irreparable harm. While it is true that we may have hurt others badly before we gave our lives to the Lord, His Word says that "He gives us back the years that the swarming locusts have eaten" (Joel 2:25). What was lost because of our sin *can* be forgiven and renewed! I have seen countless lives restored by God's power. And He will do no less in your life if you allow Him His rightful place in your life.

As long as you keep turning towards God every time you fall or disobey, you are in the right place. When the negative thoughts come, it is our responsibility to take our minds captive and replace our old mindset with God's Word. Remember, each choice we make is extremely important, as we are either moving towards the Lord, or away from Him. There is no such thing as being neutral with God ((Matthew 12:30). Don't run from His scrutiny, or His intense love for you. If we stay in intimate, daily contact with our Savior, He will keep us from deliberate sin and we will then be free of guilt (Psalm 19:13).

- What are two things you can begin to do today in order to gain freedom from your guilt?

Pray for the Holy Spirit to illuminate the "lurking" sins in your life (Psalm 19:12-13). Sometimes, we have a blind spot when it comes to our faults. We tend to see the sin in others' lives, while ignoring our own (Matthew 7:1-5). Ask for God's strength and power to overcome your disobedience. If you are not genuinely sorry, tell Him that, too! Ask Him to change the desires of your heart, so that you will want to live the life He has for you. Continue to seek the Lord every day. And don't berate yourself if you don't change overnight.

Ask God for the wisdom and power to train your mind so your guilty feelings can be released. Genuine confession is not just mouthing the words, but having the intention of changing and then allowing God to make the necessary changes in our lives. Each time we ask for forgiveness with a truly sorry heart, He supernaturally cleanses us (Psalm 51:1-17). The deeper and more often we seek Him, the more we are transformed into the likeness of Jesus! We don't fully understand this process, and the work He does in us is far beyond our own ability. But the Bible says that we are able to overcome, and we can believe this because God's Word is eternal, always true, and absolutely trustworthy.

It's time to allow His sacrifice to wash away our old thoughts. *He suffered so that we would no longer have to relive our ugly past and live in our sorrow.* He deserves our restored lives! Only as we let Him change our hearts and minds, can He reveal His glory through us to this suffering world.

Feeling remorse without change makes us victims and leads to blaming others. But genuine repentance results in a changed heart, a changed attitude, and changed actions.
We really can experience freedom from our guilt.

REFLECTION

1. Do you have unresolved guilt in your life? This can include feelings about your spouse, original family, children, or someone else you may have hurt in the past.

2. Ask yourself why you feel the need to hold onto these old feelings.

3. Do you think that by holding onto your guilty feelings, you are lessening the pain of the one you hurt?

4. Do you **want** to be set free from your guilt? (The answer to this question will take some thought. Your automatic response will probably be YES! But many times, we are afraid to let go of feelings that have become such a familiar part of us).

5. Do you **believe** that Jesus can set you free from these old thoughts and feelings? If so, how are you going to begin allowing the Holy Spirit's power to set you free?

NOTES

HOLINESS

What does the word *'holy'* mean to you? Do you think of a far-off God who is too good to rub shoulders with humanity? Or maybe you think it's just an old fashioned word that is only used to describe 'special' people. Perhaps it brings to mind others who spend time praying all day, but they live apart from the rest of the world. So what is holiness? Is there a 'prerequisite' for holiness? And how does one live a 'holy' life?

Our Special Purpose

First, let's find out what holiness means. The Hebrew language, in which the Old Testament is written, describes holiness as something or someone that is 'set apart' 'dedicated', or 'sacred'. It also means 'to clean, or to purify'. Soon after God created mankind, He chose the nation of Israel as His beloved people. He called them to 'consecrate' or devote, their very lives to Him. He wanted His love and power reflected *through* them, so that people outside of the faith would see God's glory (Exodus 6:6-9).

Many run from this whole idea of becoming holy, thinking that it is impossible to attain. To some, it just sounds like a lot of hard work, because doing their 'own thing' is so much easier. People often believe that a relationship with God will mean having to change everything in their lives. And others think that living a life of dedication to God will be 'just plain boring'.

But God's holiness has never changed, and it is still used to describe the life that He calls every Christian to live (Romans 12:1). In fact, throughout the Bible, He calls His people to 'be holy, as He is holy' (Leviticus 11:44-45). Before we are saved, we are incapable of overcoming our sinful nature. But because of the power of the Holy Spirit, we can now *choose* to live a life of purity (Romans 15:16). Of course we won't be perfect this side of heaven, but God promises to cleanse us if we allow Him dominion over our lives. And notice, it says to *be* holy, which implies a certain responsibility on our part (2 Peter 3:11-14).

You're not alone!

Christianity is the only religion in the world in which we do not have to live out our faith alone, or by our own effort. God is more than willing to help us achieve the life He calls us to live! He is alive and He has the power to create; therefore He is the only God who has the ability to infuse His creation with new life. In fact, Philippians 2:13 says that God is working in us, giving us the *desire* to obey Him and the *power* to do what pleases Him! We cannot live a life of holiness in our own strength – and that is the beauty of our Lord. *He* is the One to change us from the inside out. Our responsibility is to get close to Him and to *allow* Him to change us.

Of course, God the Father, God the Son, and God the Holy Spirit are the only absolutely holy beings in the universe. But what's astounding is that the Lord imparts *His* holiness to *us* when we trust in Jesus to be our Savior (Titus 3:3-8 and 2 Peter 1:3-4)!

It's true that our personal choices to attain holiness will require discipline, but the benefits of a godly life far outweigh doing whatever we want. What we don't realize is that the life we live apart from God literally enslaves us to our sinful nature (2 Peter

2:18-22). We may *think* we're free when we are not living under God's authority, but we are deceiving ourselves (Galatians 5:16-17). The truth is, we will never be more satisfied and content than when we turn ourselves over to the Lord; because in return, we will receive His joy, peace, love, and hope.

God's desire to make us holy is one of the primary reasons Christ died for us – so the gap between God and ourselves could be bridged (Ephesians 1:3-8). Jesus wiped the stain of our sin away so we could be close to God, who is *perfectly holy* (Colossians 1:21-22). He went to great lengths to be in relationship with us, so we could live with Him now and forever!

As if Jesus hadn't done enough for us, He also sacrificed His lifeblood so that we would be able to approach God's Throne of grace boldly (Hebrews 4:16). We can come before the Master of the universe without fear of rejection. There is no 'red tape' or scepter required for us to have an intimate relationship with our God. Just think - we can't even do that with earthly kings!

- Do you feel comfortable approaching God?
- Do you think He is too busy to hear and respond to your prayers?
- Do you feel like God is so holy that He wouldn't want to have anything to do with you?

The Temple of God

God allows us many blessings and privileges when we choose to live according to His precepts. One of the most amazing truths of the Christian life is that *we are the Temple of the Holy Spirit* (1 Corinthians 3:16-17)! In the Old Testament, the very first Temple on earth was built. It was the most sacred spot on earth, because it housed

God Himself (1 Kings 8:10 and Habakkuk 2:20)! And miraculously, we as Christians are also housing God, the Holy Spirit, in our lives when we accept Jesus into our hearts.

Jesus Himself is the 'cornerstone' of this Temple (1 Peter 2:4). Amazingly, it was prophesied almost 660 years earlier that He would be this tested and stable Cornerstone (Isaiah 28:16)! The 'cornerstone' is the most important piece of a building, as it holds the structure together. And similarly, Christ is the Head of the Church, holding her together (Ephesians 5:23).

As we continue to let go of the past and allow God to heal us, our 'temple' becomes more and more inviting to the Holy Spirit (Ephesians 2:19-22). As we come to know God more intimately, we will gain a new desire to protect our lives from sin, because our love for the Lord will deepen, giving us the desire to please Him even more. And we'll soon come to a place where we will not want to grieve Him (Ephesians 4:30).

<u>We are Priests of the Most High God</u>

Although there were many priests in the Hebrew nation, there was only one that was called the 'High Priest'. He was the sole person who was allowed to enter into the most sacred room in the Temple, called the 'Holy of Holies'. He did this once a year, to offer a sacrifice for the sins of the Jewish people. This ritual was a foreshadow of Jesus Christ, who became *our* High Priest (Hebrews 2:17; 3:1; 4:15 and 10:19-21). He is the One who has given us access into the Holy Room of God Himself. He is also the Chief Mediator and Advocate between us and God, thereby fulfilling His priestly duties (1Timothy 2:3-6). And as God, He is blameless and holy, just as He calls us to be (Hebrews 7:26).

It is essential for us to read and understand the Old Testament, because it is a 'prototype' of our faith today. For example, we as Christians are *priests of God* (1 Peter 2:5, 9; Revelation 1:5-6 and Revelation 5:9-10). This is a high calling of privilege and responsibility! As priests, our job entails continually offering sacrifices of praise to God, and surrendering to His Kingship. We are also to proclaim the glory of His name and the beauty of His character to other people. We are called to share what we have with those in need, as this is also a pleasing sacrifice to God (Hebrews 13:15-16).

- How does it make you feel, knowing that as a believer, you are the Temple of the Holy Spirit and a Priest to the Most High God?

We are standing on Holy Ground

The Hebrew people were constantly aware that as they related to God, they were *standing on holy ground* (Exodus 3:5). Their faith was woven into the fabric of their daily lives, so they knew that they were in God's presence at all times. As believers, we need to be mindful of this important truth when we are in relationship with the Lord, as well.

We've seen that Jesus has given us free access to God's throne. But this grace did not come cheaply. We need to uphold an attitude of reverence when we come to Him. Far too many Christians today treat God casually, as if He were just their 'buddy'. Remember, He is altogether holy, and as such, He deserves our absolute adoration, respect, and awe. After all, He IS the King of kings and Lord of lords (1 Timothy 1:17; 1 Timothy 6:15-16; Revelation 17:14)! And He is the *eternal* and *all powerful* God!

- What is your attitude towards God when you pray?

What happens if we continue to live in an unholy manner?

We have learned that holiness is one of God's main objectives for our lives. When we continue to live in sin, the Bible says that we are not disobeying human rules, but we are rejecting God Himself (1 Thessalonians 4:7-8). All we have to do is look around today to see how fully sin has permeated our society. And it's interesting to see that our culture is not the first in history to have such widespread disobedience. We find several startling similarities with Israel in 700 B.C. to our America today (Isaiah 59:1-14). And civilizations as powerful as the Roman Empire have fallen, not because of lack of might, but as a direct result of their rampant immorality. Clearly, when we worship and tolerate unholy things, we BECOME unholy! God calls us to be morally upright. And He wants us to be salt and light to this dying world, so the unsaved will be attracted to Him (Matthew 5:13-16).

It's important to realize that our desire for holiness is a direct byproduct of our passion for Jesus. And we will most certainly lose our passion for Him if we continue to allow sin to override our relationship with Him. We like to think we are immune from falling away from God, but our hearts can be deceived and hardened. Isaiah 29:13 speaks of those who used to love and obey God, but ended up 'honoring' Him only with their words. Sadly, their hearts were completely removed from Him. In fact, the entire Old Testament is a story about the Israelites vacillating from loving God to turning away from Him.

By the time Jesus came, this human condition hadn't changed much, because He spoke the same words 700 years later in Matthew 15:8-9! And He would probably say the exact same thing to us if He were alive on earth today. Even though we may continue to do the outward things – like going to church or attending Christian events, our desire for Him will surely fade if we do not choose to remain holy. And only heart-ache will follow.

It is a slippery slope, but usually not a quick descent. It may *seem* like suddenly, we 'wake up' and realize we have become 'fake' Christians. But this lifestyle is made one decision at a time – by choosing our selfishness over the things of the Lord. We begin to lose our interest in church, Christian people, God's Word, and anything else that relates to Jesus.

We can even slide into the camp that rejects Him if we continue to refuse His headship in our lives. There is no middle ground with God. That's why He calls us to *guard our hearts* above all else (Proverbs 4:23; Proverbs 7:2-3; and Philippians 4:7). Additionally, only as we **continue** in the ways of the Lord will HE guard us from the evil one (2 Thessalonians 3:1-5 and 2 Peter 3:17-18).

Taking a frequent 'inventory' of your spiritual health is imperative. A great scripture that allows us a closer look at the quality of our relationship with God is found in Mark 4:3-20. The parable of the four soils shows us how deep our faith really is. Interestingly, we can have different 'soils' in our lives at the same time. And we may have different soils at different times of our lives. We may give God one part of our lives (fertile soil), such as our time, money and talent. But at the same time, we may choose to keep Him out of our secret life - our addictions, or our sinful habits (rocky soil).

We may also go through times when we don't feel very close to God, as if we're in the wilderness. While it's natural to experience an ebb and flow in our relationship, it is imperative that we continue to meet with God so that we don't lose our affection for Him altogether.

Keep a close eye on your attitudes and behavior! If we continue to walk further away from Jesus, we are putting ourselves at risk (Hebrews 6:4-6 and 2 Peter 2:19-22). While Jesus does intercede to the Father when we *occasionally* sin, we are not to live a *lifestyle* of selfish living (2 Corinthians 12:19-21). If we call ourselves Christians but continually live ungodly lives, we are liars and God is not really in us (1 John 2:3-6 and 3:7-10).

- What kind of life are you living right now? Do you feel like you are conquering your sin and selfishness?
- Or are you overwhelmed by your fleshly nature?
- If you are living only for yourself, you can begin by praying for the *desire* to change, so you can begin making godly choices.

<u>What does a life of holiness entail?</u>

1. *Giving our whole lives to God.*

This may sound like an impossibility, but just like anything in life that we really want to do, we set our focus on what we want to accomplish. We think about it, plan for it, and set aside less important tasks, so we can achieve our goal.

Being in relationship with God is no different. When we make lifestyle choices that ensure our intimacy with Jesus, <u>His</u> desire for our life unfolds into a perfect plan. Again, we need to keep pressing into God and His Word, even when we may not feel like it.

As our relationship with Him grows, He will ask for more and more of our lives. We must work towards keeping our minds and hearts on His purposes. The only way we will reap the benefits of God's plan is to wholeheartedly move in His direction. God wants total dedication from our lives, not half-hearted commitment (Deuteronomy 6:4-9).

2. *Getting rid of the past*

We cannot continue to look back, longing for our old life. Genesis 19:17 and 26 shows us a perfect example of this behavior. Continuing to desire people or things from our ungodly past is spiritual suicide, because we will never attain a holy life if we have our hearts and minds set in two camps. Jesus said that anyone who continues to desire his old life is not fit for God's kingdom (Luke 9:62)!

The Bible says that we cannot live the Christian life 'on the fence'; we cannot serve God and 'self' successfully (Matthew 6:24). This scripture uses the word 'money', but the idea here is allowing **any** person, passion, hobby, or goal to be put above our desire for the Lord.

And James 1:6-8 talks about the double minded person. When we have two opposing mindsets, it will bring doubt to our minds. Going to church on Sundays and Wednesdays, but watching and reading ungodly material during the week, is an example of living a double-minded life. Being a Christian involves living for God every day of the week, and making Him part of every single decision we make. The Lord says that we should not expect our relationship with Him to bring fruit if we live a wishy-washy life, full of indecision about our commitment to Him. If we are living this way, we need to repent and humble ourselves, so that we will receive honor from the Lord, not the world (James 4:7-10).

We must realize that we can't pick and choose between the things we want from God and the things we want to keep from our previous lifestyle. We may have to leave people, things, or places that keep us bound to our past. We have to accept the Cross along with the crown, and judgment as well as mercy. We must count the cost of serving Jesus and be willing to abandon everything that has brought us security in the past (Luke 9:23-26).

This does not mean we have to sell all of our possessions or rigorously refrain from any pleasure! But we do need to live a life that keeps us from every distraction that leads us away from the call that God has on our lives. If we choose to live a lifestyle of obedience, we will find that dedicating ourselves to God brings us what we are truly looking for - peace, joy, contentment, hope, direction, security and love. This does *not* mean we won't have problems – but it does mean we will be more positively adjusted to be able to handle the ups and downs in our lives.

3. Growing in holiness

In order to genuinely grow into a life of holiness, we need to immerse ourselves in the Word of God. This is **essential** for our growth and maturation in Christ. Ephesians 5:26 says that Jesus gave up His life to make the church (us) holy and clean, and that we are washed by baptism and *God's Word.*

2 Timothy 3:16-17 lists many virtues that are developed by reading God's Word:

-It is inspired (meaning 'God-breathed'). It is therefore completely trustworthy and solid, which brings genuine security to our lives.
-It is useful to teach us what is true
-It allows us to realize what is wrong in our lives
-It straightens us out
-It teaches us to do what is right
-It is God's way of preparing us in every way
-It fully equips us to do every good thing God wants us to do

Hebrews 4:12-14 says that the Bible is *alive*, and is able to change us, because it exposes our innermost thoughts and desires. Also, our minds are renewed by the Spirit of God through the reading of the Word (Romans 12:2). And remember, only as we *do* what God instructs, will we receive the blessing He promises (James 2:17-20).

- Does living a life of holiness sound appealing to you? Or does it sound boring?
- Maybe you are rejecting holiness because you feel it would tie you down and keep you from doing what you want to do.

So how do we become holy?

Hebrews 10:14 says that by Christ's offering and shed blood, God perfected forever those whom He is making holy. Sounds like a bunch of mumbo jumbo until you understand what it means. When we accept Christ and His atonement (payment) for our sins, we are immediately made pure in our spirit –which is what the 'perfected forever' part means. And when Jesus comes into our hearts, we are born again - we come alive spiritually (Romans 6:1-11). If we died today, after having received salvation, we would be with Jesus forever.

However, our flesh still needs work, which is the '*making* holy' part of the scripture we just read. This is the *process* of being made holy, and it happens only when we cooperate with the Father by allowing *our* choices to line up with *His* truth and desires (1 Peter 1:13-25).

It is God's responsibility to purify us by His Word (John 17:17) and by His Holy Spirit. He also purifies us by His blood (1 Peter 1:2). God does not want us to come into heaven by the skin of our teeth! He *wants* to give us new life (Ephesians 2:10). He *wants* us to have the power to do as He asks. He *wants* us to be filled with His Spirit, so that we can overcome our sin. His desire is that we become so passionate about Him that we offer hope and love to this dying world. And His plan is for us to influence others in a powerful way, so that they can know Him too.

Even though God does the real transforming work in our lives, we are still in a partnership with Him. As we make wise decisions to live Christ's way, we become stronger in spirit. It's the same idea as when we physically exercise. The more we do it, the easier it is, and the more conditioned we become. As we exercise our spiritual muscles by choosing God's ways over ours, it becomes much easier to stay pure. This is the secret of achieving a holy life in Christ - *As we decide to make right and godly choices, God empowers us to obey His voice* (Romans 6:12-16).

1 Peter 1:13-15 says that we should:

Begin to exercise self-control

Think clearly

Obey God

Not slip back into our old ways of life

- Are you making choices in your daily life that reflect your relationship with Christ?
- Or are you continuing to gossip, complain, overindulge, act ungrateful, remain in ungodly relationships, and continuing to allow sexual sin in your life, etc?

<u>Control yourself!</u>

Our lives should increasingly show freedom from the corruption of sin. 1 John 3:1-3 says we are to keep OURSELVES pure, because we have the blessed hope of eternity with Jesus. This life is our dress rehearsal for heaven (1 John 2:15-17)! We maintain our holiness by *staying away* from our known temptations to sin. We are to *cleanse ourselves* from everything that can sully our bodies, minds, words, attitudes, or spirits (2 Corinthians 7:1). We are to *work towards* purity, in reverence to God.

Interestingly, holiness is not just the absence of sin. We gain freedom from our old life by not only turning away *from* sin, but turning *towards* Christ! It is an attitude in which we *actively* seek Jesus deeply, continuously and fervently. Remember, we are victorious because of the Holy Spirit living within us, but it is our **choices** that allow Him to do His perfect work. He is a Gentleman, and will not force Himself on you. And be prepared - this new way of life will create an excitement and desire for God that will be overwhelming in nature (Romans 15:13)!

In this process of meeting daily with God through prayer, praise and the Bible, we *become* holy and set apart. Then He can use us for *His* glory. This is the purpose for which we were created, and we are never so alive as when we are living in His power and for His purposes! We have been rescued from our enemies *so that we can serve God without fear, in holiness and righteousness forever* (Luke 1:74-75)!

- Are you willing to set quality time aside every day, just to meet with God?

<u>God adores us!</u>

And lastly, we need to understand *how much God loves us and wants us to be holy* so we can receive His entire blessing. He wants us to be set apart so that we can be a source of hope to this dark world. Ephesians 1:4 says that before God even made the earth, He loved us and chose us to be holy and without fault in His eyes. As a result of the Holy Spirit's work, we are cleansed by Jesus' blood and receive the power to obey Him. The more we come into genuine fellowship with the Lord, the more we will be purified. We will receive more of God's special favor, and experience more of His wonderful peace. And the beautiful part of Jesus' sacrifice is that it allows us to come to the Father not only reverently, but intimately, as God is also our Daddy (Romans 8:15).

- Are you absolutely sure that you are going to heaven?

Experiencing change

If you want to begin living more passionately for the Lord, this is the place to start. Remember, as we become more like Jesus through obedience to His Word, God's purpose for our lives becomes *our* goals as well. His desire is for every area of our lives to come under the power of His Holy Spirit. Allowing Him to wash us and make us holy will result in the rich fruit that comes from a life of purity. We will experience joy, peace, love, kindness, gentleness, hope and self-control. After all, this is what the human heart is truly looking for! And as we are changed, we will be able to influence the unsaved, so they can have eternal life, too.

God's qualities in our life should make us different. People should sense that we are not of this world (John 17:13-19). Think about that in your life. Because of your level of commitment to God, do people want to meet Jesus, or do they even know you are a Christian?

\- - - - - - - - -

My prayer for you all is that you will develop a burning desire for Jesus. That you would search for Him **daily**, through prayer and His Word, for YOURSELVES! I want you to WANT to meet with Him at every opportunity! And I pray that you will want to please Him with your entire life. Remember, there is no way to pay our Savior back for all He has done for us and all He has given us, except choosing to give Him our lives. Turning our sin, guilt, fears, dreams and goals over to Him involves making choices that will honor holiness and righteousness over our sin and our flesh. In this alone, we will influence others to come to Him and we will then bring glory to our wonderful Father.

REFLECTION

1. Remember the parable of the four soils? Think about which soil you are in the following areas:
   a. God. Let's say God asks you to do something that is not what you really want to do – how do you respond?
   b. Work or school. Are you known as a complainer, party animal, or gossiper? Or are people glad to have you around because of your joy, integrity, and cooperative spirit?
   c. Relationships. Are you known for extending grace to others, especially when they are weak or slower at understanding? How about the way you treat housekeepers, clerks, or other people who aren't in high positions? Are you known for your forgiveness in your marriage, and to family members, church members, or co-workers?
   d. Ourselves. Are we courageous enough to dig deep into our minds, hearts and souls to allow God to reveal our filth? This is the only way to heal and change so that God can make us holy. God wants all of your secret parts – your attitudes of selfishness, pride, and self-sufficiency. Your addictions and idols. Your fears and hopes. Your desires and limitations. Write your answers to these questions below.

2. Are we to become holy in our own power?

3. What are some ways we change when we accept Christ?

4. What are some of the fruits of holiness?

5. What are you willing to start doing today to become more like Jesus?

NOTES

HUMILITY

Humility.

Hmmm. That must mean weakness. Doormat material. Whimps. Being embarrassed in front of others. Putting myself down....

Now why would I want any part of humility?

Actually, many people don't even know what humility means. And it's certainly hard to find this quality in our culture today. We are a nation that is obsessed with those at the top - the best, the most beautiful, the most fit, the smartest, and the most powerful. The very word 'humility' causes people to believe that if they are humble, they will get nowhere in life. Eating 'humble pie' means that you have cowered and lost. And we often think of 'the humble' as being the poor, despised, and downtrodden in this world.

Humility is....

Humility *is* a picture of someone who draws their strength, peace, and direction from the Lord. It's one who knows their strengths and limitations, and still let's God be the Boss of their lives. And the one who is so confident and secure in their position that they don't need to seek status, or exert their self-imposed power in every situation.

The biblical definition of humility is far different than the self-centered qualities that our society embraces. Far from being weak, humility really means 'strength under control'. The English dictionary describes humility as being 'modest' or 'respectful'. It's really a *lifestyle* attitude of putting others before ourselves. And it requires great fortitude and self-control, because people that are humble before God consistently act in ways that are contrary to their sinful nature. They choose to love when they are hated. They decide to share their time, talent, and money, instead of hoarding everything for themselves. And they have God's power and courage to do good to others, even when they are faced with evil. It's no wonder that we have trouble finding those who display genuine humility.

Being humble is also the ability to acknowledge that God is the Master Controller of the Universe and we are not. You may say "Of course He is!" But our actions really do speak louder than our words. For example, how many times have we thought "I am the only one who can do my job right". Or, "I'm the only one who parents my child properly". The list of ways that we think we are indispensible could go on and on. The point is, we often believe that we are far too important, as if we really do control all circumstances. It takes far greater character to admit that we need God's help to conquer our selfishness and to display genuine love. Humility is the purposeful act of turning our will, our minds, and our hearts over to Him, rather than living in our own strength (Deuteronomy 10:12-21).

Human beings usually don't like to be treated negatively or disrespectfully. We react a lot more positively if we are treated with respect and kindness. For example, don't you enjoy it when someone let's you go first in line, or in traffic? Doesn't it make you feel good when someone offers to help you without you even asking? This attitude creates a spirit of kinship, as opposed to one of competition. Thinking of others *before* ourselves is the essence of humility.

- Can you think of some ways that your humility is evident?
- Are there things that you can start doing to become more humble?

Humility is not....

Humility is **not** letting people run all over you. It is **not** humiliation. And it's not serving others to the point of ignoring our own needs. The opposite of humility is arrogance – also called pride. Arrogance says 'I can and I will'. In fact, this is the very attitude that got Satan kicked out of heaven (Isaiah 14:12-14). Many people live their lives out of sheer determination, with a blatant disregard for God. It's 'their way or the highway'. They are defined by their achievements and push through life getting their way no matter what.

While there is nothing wrong with being successful, and feeling good about your accomplishments, those who take complete credit for the success in their lives without asking or thanking God for His help tend to develop a false attitude of superiority. Furthermore, relying on ourselves and our circumstances alone leads to an artificial sense of security, because people and circumstances change daily. Nothing in the world stays the same except for God Himself (Hebrews 1:10-12). Therefore, He is the only One who deserves our absolute trust and devotion. The truth is, we lack genuine wisdom when we ignore Him, and we become utter fools instead (Psalm 14:1 and Romans 3:10-18).

Additionally, when we willfully stand against God, we miss out on all that He has planned for our lives. If we insist on living only by our rules and desires, we will lose the blessings He has in store for us. We will also fail to go through the essential times of healthy testing and pruning that He designs for us. Seeking Him and trusting Him leads to a life that is far more satisfying than you can even imagine (Proverbs 3:5-8).

- Do you think you rely more on yourself, or more on God?

<u>You're missing out!</u>

You may be saying right about now that your life is fine, and it certainly doesn't need to be humbled under God. Maybe you have a wonderful marriage, home, job, and children. However, as people continue along their own 'path' without God, they usually find themselves disenchanted with their accomplishments, abilities, and acquisitions. Often they find themselves asking if this is 'all there is to life'. You know, the "What's my purpose?", "Where am I going?", and "Why am I here?" sort of questions. People may think they already have all they need without Jesus, but they don't realize that <u>so</u> much is missing from their lives.

When we are new to faith in Christ, we may be reluctant to allow Him control. But this relationship is built over time, and if we stay committed to Him, He will continue to prove His trustworthiness through our trials. As we give Him a little part of ourselves at a time, we start to see what He can and will do, *in* us, *through* us, and *for* us. We'll come to understand that He is reliable and always has our very best interest at heart. And soon, we will realize that He loves us so intensely that He would never hurt us or forsake us. He is the very best kind of Husband (Isaiah 54:4-5), Friend (John 15:15), and Father (Romans 8:15).

And if we have been in relationships where we have been treated harshly or even abusively, we may be even more hesitant to turn our wills, emotions, and souls over to Jesus. We may have worked very hard to gain control over our lives after these types of hardships. In this situation, the last thing we probably want to do is give any of our newfound power over to anyone, including God Himself.

But we will never be complete without living in communion with God. He designed us that way. So, if you are looking for 'more' out of life, then the Lord has **you** in mind.

The meaning of life is only truly satisfied when we are in relationship with the One who created us. He understands us intimately, and He loves us passionately. He has a master plan for your life that includes joy, peace, hope, and purpose. He is only waiting for you to ask Him into your life.

- Do you think your life is centered around Christ?
- Or do you run your own life and only let Him in when you feel like it?
- It will be easier to answer this question if you evaluate:

  how much time you spend thinking about Him

  how often you spend time reading the Bible

  how much time you spend praying

  and what you spend your time, talent, and money on

But I feel so betrayed

Maybe you have entrusted yourself to God and then something bad happened to you. Your first response might be "God, I thought you were going to be there for me"! In reality, He IS there for you, right by your side. Just because we are in submission to Him does not mean He is going to take away the difficult situations in our lives. In fact, He often uses these very circumstances to draw us closer to Him. In reality, you would probably be going through the same trials even if you weren't in relationship with Him! Only as you continue trusting in God, will you find a peace and a strength in your trials that is clearly not your own (Philippians 4:6-7).

And don't forget that in the end, every single person who ever lived WILL humble themselves and bow their knee to God – either out of love or fear (Romans 14:11). It's our choice – and there are only two options. As we humble ourselves before Him now, we can live a life that not only pleases Him, but we will share in the privilege of influencing others, so they can also receive the goodness that God so richly supplies to the submitted believer.

- Do you believe that God is really present through your hardships? How can you tell?

<u>What does living a life of humility involve?</u>

Many people think that repentance is the first step to coming to Christ. But it is actually humility, because we have to realize our need for a Savior even before we ask Him into our hearts and decide to turn from our sin. When we humble ourselves, we are admitting that we really can't handle our lives in the best way possible. Giving the reins over to God can be frightening, but we are never wiser than when we bow before the King of Creation (Proverbs 9:10 and 11:2).

Jesus Himself says in Matthew 18:1-4 that we are to humble ourselves like children in order to come into the kingdom of God. He used children as an example, because they have no problem acknowledging that they are utterly dependent on adults. In the same way, coming to Jesus in faith requires an attitude of childlike dependence if we are to live the way God wants us to. Without humility, we will be continually fighting God for the 'power seat'. And this will surely make us miserable in our Christian walk.

Does this mean we are we supposed to grovel before God, begging Him for our every need? Are we supposed to cringe before Him in fear? The answer to both of these questions is a resounding no! God knows our every need before we ask (Matthew 6:25-34). Actually, when we choose to be in a passionate relationship with Him, He delights in answering our prayers. And it is the Lord's desire for us to be filled with confidence because we trust in Him! (Psalm 37:3-5). He went to the cross because of His great love for us; so we would know that we are of immeasurable worth to Him.

But healthy confidence and true stability are only possible when we deeply understand that *Jesus* is the anchor of our souls and *He* is our Great Shepherd (Hebrews 6:19 and John 10:11). When we believe in His awesome power, we come to realize that *He* is the reason we are safe; it is not our human accomplishments that bring us security.

Remember, everything we do in this world will either last or burn. All of our money, jobs, toys, houses, clothes and cars will be meaningless on judgment day. If our work is solely to bring ourselves glory and pleasure, we will stand before the God of the universe empty handed. Maybe this doesn't seem very important to you now, but you do not want to stand at the gate of eternity and find out you are going to hell because you were too proud to submit to Christ. The fact is, <u>only</u> the things we do in God's power, and for His purposes, will bring eternal benefit and honor (Job 22).

- Is your confidence built on your own accomplishments, or is it based on what God is doing in your life?

<u>Oh no! Not submission!</u>

Humbling ourselves also involves submission, which is another word that many people don't understand. While the meaning of submission is 'to surrender or yield', biblical submission doesn't have anything to do with being a pushover. In fact, we see all throughout the gospels that Jesus had no problem calling people out on their sin (Matthew 7:5; Matthew 23:13; Luke 6:42 and Luke 13:16)! Just like humbling ourselves, choosing to submit takes great self-control. It is a decision of our will and takes concerted effort. It is a choice; one that is made with our hearts, minds, and souls.

We are to <u>clothe ourselves</u> with mercy, humility, kindness, gentleness and patience (Ephesians 4:1-6 and Colossians 3:12-15). This kind of submission implies an act of purpose, not the idea of being forced or shamed to perform. By *choosing* to act like

Jesus, we show others the qualities that are only present when we are authentically Christ-centered. And the Holy Spirit promises to help us obey the Word of God, after we make the choice to do so.

When we submit ourselves to the Lord, we literally *give Him permission* to be in control of our lives. It is certainly not a silly, no-brainer decision made in the folly of the moment. Submitting ourselves to God takes careful consideration and forethought.

- Which areas in your life do you still need to submit to God?

Turning from our sin

Humility also involves a turning away from temptation and choosing to make godly choices. In fact, God promises blessing only IF we obey Him (2 Chronicles 7:14-16).

If my people, who are called by My name
Will HUMBLE themselves
And pray
And seek My face
And turn from their wicked ways,

THEN

I will hear from heaven!
I will forgive their sins!
And I will heal their land! (the 'land' includes our personal lives as well as our country)

Remember, our ways are *not* the Lord's ways (Isaiah 55:8-9). He is all powerful (omnipotent), all knowing (omniscient) and ever present (omnipresent). However smart or clever or confident we *think* we are without Him, we are completely deceiving ourselves if we fail to walk in His ways!

<u>That ugly old monster</u>

We've already learned that the opposite of humility is arrogance. And the Bible has plenty to say on this subject. We have all probably heard the saying "Pride goes before destruction and haughtiness before a fall" (Proverbs 16:18). I think that the word 'fall' is used here because the proud have a tendency to elevate themselves too highly, and a downward plunge is the only direction they can go! Interestingly, one of the root words for humility is 'base' or 'lowly', which implies that the humble one is solidly on the ground and cannot be easily shaken or moved!

Pride eventually brings us to a state of humiliation, but humility brings us honor (Proverbs 29:23). We may read this and think "Well, what about all those people that are having so much fun because they are rich and beautiful? They aren't living a life of humility, but they have everything and they seem so happy!" Actually, it only takes a closer look to find that there are plenty of ruined lives as a result of all the 'fun' they are experiencing. Again, being proud brings us ruin, but honor is ours if we submit ourselves to God (Proverbs 18:12).

It may seem contrary to your thinking, but God's Word makes it clear that an attitude of servant-hood brings us much more satisfaction than being haughty and selfish. It also pleases God when we choose to give our lives away to others. Make no mistake - the proud will surely be brought down (Isaiah 2:11). And the humble *will* inherit the earth (Matthew 5:5). Those that are seen as the 'greatest' in this life will be the 'least' when judgment comes (Matthew 19:28-30). However, God promises that if we *choose* to be the least, we will be exalted in the end (Luke 14:7-11).

Some of God's truths are hard to swallow. But Jesus says that those who have given nothing for the Kingdom of God will be in for a surprise when He returns (Matthew 25:31-46). If we call ourselves Christians, but we are self-centered and give very little for His purposes, only a little will be given to us (Matthew 25:14-28). The only thing that absolutely matters while we are alive on this earth is what we believe about Jesus and what we do for Him (Matthew 16:24-28).

And speaking of pride, it's interesting to see that it is right up there in the 'sin' lists - along with murder, greed, cruelty, and those who hate God (Romans 1:28-32 and 2 Timothy 3:1-5)! The Lord says that He literally *hates* pride (Proverbs 8:13). So, when we proudly reject His authority, we are actually choosing to live in the enemies' camp (Matthew 12:30 and James 4:4-10). The truth is, we will be humbled either way – either by our own choices or by our circumstances (Matthew 23:11-12).

Most of us wouldn't use the word 'proud' to describe ourselves. However, if you are not submitted to the Lord Jesus Christ, then you are really saying that you know how to manage your life more skillfully than God. And that is the purest form of pride!

- How much time and/or money do you spend helping people outside of your family? This will help you determine how much of a humble servant you really are.

Our Perfect Example

Jesus' life was the perfect example of humility. He could have called a hundred thousand angels to His aid in a second (Matthew 26:53), but He chose to relinquish much of His power as God so that He could humble Himself for our sake. Philippians 2:5-11 is the scripture that most beautifully illustrates this point:

Your attitude should be the same that Christ Jesus had.
Though He was God, He laid aside His mighty power and glory;
He took the humble position of a slave and appeared in human form.
In human form, He obediently humbled Himself even further
By dying a criminal's death on a cross.
Because of this, God raised Him up to the heights of heaven
And gave Him a name above every name
So that at the name of Jesus, every knee will bow and every tongue
Will confess that Jesus Christ is Lord
To the glory of God the Father.

So you see, even God Himself chose to be humble! He lowered Himself *on purpose*. He knew He would be spit upon, abused, and misunderstood. And yet He deliberately restrained Himself, so that we would gain the benefits of His sacrifice. But notice that the reward for His faithful service is eternal glory and power. And the amazing thing is, that is our reward, too (Ephesians 3:6 and Revelation 21:7). He demonstrated immense 'strength under control', and He is our example to follow.

Jesus was the ultimate Servant, which is a 'humble server' (Matthew 20:26-28). Don't be surprised - giving our lives away to help others will oftentimes feel very contrary to our natural will. But we show great strength of character when we refrain from our selfishness in order to serve others. Again, those who exalt themselves will *be* humbled, but those who *humble themselves* will be exalted (1 Peter 5:5-6). Only as we bow down before the Lord and admit our dependence on Him will He lift us up and give us honor.

God's promised blessings for the humble

What are our promises from God when we *do* humble ourselves and submit to Him?

There are so many benefits to humbling ourselves and obeying God that they cannot all be listed in this study. However, if we read Psalm 34, we will see a beautiful picture of the blessings that will be ours if we choose to be in relationship with the Lord. He will protect us, listen to us, teach us, protect us, guard us, and save us. What's even more wonderful is that God wants this connection with us even more than we do! And we know this because He died for us while we were still sinners (Romans 5:8).

Another benefit to putting ourselves under the authority of God is that His Holy Spirit gives us the power to resist the devil. Actually, the Bible says that Satan will FLEE from us as we stand against his attacks (Ephesians 6:12-17 and James 4:4-10)! In addition, as we draw close to God, He will draw close to us. He is **always** waiting for us to run to Him. But He won't force us -we need to desire Him and want Him to direct our hearts and minds. And as His Spirit draws us in, we have the choice to either turn to Him or turn away.

God promises to dwell within the lives of those who are humble (Isaiah 57:15). The thought of Him living inside of me makes me feel so amazing! I am wonderfully special and chosen (Ephesians 1:3-14)! In addition, the humble will also will be given the spiritual ability to see God at work in their lives and the lives of others (Psalm 69:32). And also, we won't have to 'muster up' our own bravery. He will give us authentic courage so that we can handle life's burdens and hardships more positively (Psalm 18:25-36).

God's promise of protection

In order to be truly successful, (and by that I mean walking on the road of God's will for our lives), we need to realize that we are full of frailties and imperfections. We all become self centered and foolish at some point. However, when God is in control of our lives, the Holy Spirit can weave in and around our lives to correct our steps (Psalm 25:8-10; 32:8-9 and Proverbs 3:5-6).

Another great benefit of submitting ourselves before God is that He promises to comfort, heal, and protect us through our troubles. He says that He will not give us more than we can handle, so whatever we are going through, we can be sure that God has decided that we *are able* to go through it (1 Corinthians 10:12-13)! God is eternal and knows everything at all times. When we place our trust and our lives under His 'wings', we are sheltered from the storms we encounter (Psalm 91). Not only that, but there are countless times that we are kept from harm without even knowing it - IF *we come under the umbrella of HIS protection* (Proverbs 30:1-6).

Those who live without Christ have only themselves and other humans to rely on. This can be frightening when we are at our wits end. All it takes is one look at this world to see the depression, anger, hopelessness and disrespect that 'doing our own thing' has brought us. On the contrary, the Christian who has an intimate relationship with the Creator of the Universe has Someone who is not only **willing** to help, but Who is absolutely **able**! He *wants* us to become more like Him. Letting go of our old thinking and our old behavior, and trusting the Lord in humility will produce fruit that is priceless and altogether lovely.

- Can you think of a time when you were humble and obedient, and God blessed you for it?

God's Refining Fire

Most of us dislike going through hard times. But when we're humbled under God's mighty hand, He will oftentimes use difficult circumstances in our lives that are *meant* to refine us. He does this because He loves us, and He wants us to be His people (Zechariah 13:9).

God actually *uses* our suffering to 'burn' off the impurities in our lives, just like a goldsmith heats up the metal to purify it. As the heat increases, an impure, filmy substance is taken off the top of the liquid metal, which is called the 'slag' or the 'dross'. What's left is only the purest metal.

The 'slag and dross' in our lives is our tendency to be selfish, to gossip, to waste our time, to indulge in mental or physical sexual sin, to be self-centered, to be greedy, to look down on others, and a host of other ungodly attitudes and behaviors. This refining process ultimately tests our character, because after the suffering, nothing is left except the pure product of *who we are*.

The Lord also allows these hardships to deepen our dependence on Him. And His glory can be shown through our trials, because He provides for us and moves in our lives in ways that are clearly not human (Psalm 86:1-13). As our Creator, He certainly knows how we function best, and what we need in order to find our greatest potential. And He knows that these precious times of testing will bring us the most joy, peace, and purpose.

- Do you allow God to mold and shape you when times of testing come?
- Do you throw a tantrum and play the victim?
- Or do you ignore His authority by insisting on doing things your own way?

<u>It's time</u>

If you have not yet placed your trust in Jesus, now is the time. Many people think they can do whatever they want for their whole lives, and then, at the last minute, make a decision for Christ just to get into heaven. But this is a lie from the devil. No man knows the hour he will be called to eternity. You may not get the chance.

If you *have* placed your faith in Christ, it's a good time to measure your level of humility. Are you truly submitting your selfish ways to Him? Are you a bright, shining example of Jesus to this lost world? Or are you only living a 'partial' life for Him? The fact is, it is imperative that you *humble yourself now.* The time is short, and it doesn't take a genius to see that this world is spinning out of control. Today is the day to harvest souls for Christ. And remember, *only* as we choose to come under God's hand, will we be able to stand against the attacks of the enemy of our souls (1 Peter 5:6-9). Living life on God's terms brings immeasurable blessings.

<u>Today</u> is the day to humble yourself and repent of your ways.

REFLECTION

1. What is humility?

2. Do we **have** to humble ourselves before God?

3. What are some of the promises God has for us if we do humble ourselves?
   Hint: Look up James 4:7, 1 Peter 5:6, and 2 Chronicles 7:14

4. Are our problems going to disappear if we humble our lives to God? Why not?

5. What is true success in this life? Why?

6. What did Jesus say about achieving 'greatness' in the kingdom of heaven?

NOTES

OBEDIENCE

Deuteronomy, Chapter 6

Does the word 'obedience' bring negative thoughts to your mind? Maybe you had parents who were too strict. Or teachers that criticized you. Perhaps it brings to mind an overbearing God who just wants to keep you from having fun. We all have different ideas when it comes to this often misunderstood concept of obedience.

We are very particular about the ways in which we choose to obey. Most of us don't have a problem obeying traffic lights or following the instructions to make our new appliances work. But tell someone that their lifestyle is revealing their disobedience to God, and you will find many people snarling in defense.

<u>Obedience means...</u>

The Hebrew word for obedience is 'shama' which means 'to hear intelligently' (I love that!) It also means 'to listen', 'to consent', 'to hear', 'to declare', and 'to be diligent'. The Greek word is 'hupakouo', meaning 'to hear' (as a subordinate), 'to listen attentively', 'to heed or conform to authority', and 'to be obedient to'.

But before we can obey, we must learn to listen. 'Hearing' is a physiological function, whereby air enters the ear canal and sound is transmitted. But 'listening' is a mental, emotional, and spiritual function. There are a multitude of people today who have no idea *how* to listen. Many are so busy talking, they find it hard to even take in information. And we've all dealt with those who 'hear' us, but they don't really *understand* what we are saying. People have trouble even sitting still so that they can listen to God speak to them. Self-examination or meditation in a quiet setting is rare. The real tragedy is that we can be so self-absorbed that we fail to take notice of others who may need our help or attention.

Obedience to God, authority, and parents seems to be a thing of the past. Instead, we have become a culture that bows only to 'self'. There was a time when people meant more than money. We respected our elders, and we had pride in our nation. Our parents weren't afraid to discipline us, which taught us how to control ourselves.

But our country was great, because it was built on the principles of scripture. In fact, almost all of the forefathers who developed our Constitution and our government were devout Christians. That's sure something we don't hear about in our history books today! But our rejection of God and His ways is precisely the reason why our country is disintegrating before our very eyes.

- Do you think you're a good listener? How can you tell?

<u>What were they thinking?</u>

The Bible is our handbook for life. But few are diligent students of its timeless wisdom and instruction. And oftentimes, the largest part of God's Word, the Old Testament, is ignored, because it is viewed as a list of rules and regulations. People that haven't even read the Bible often believe that it is a collection of old dusty poems, words and names that seem impossible to pronounce, and a God that is always mad!

But taken in its entirety, the first two thirds of the Bible is a story about Israel, the nation whom God Himself formed and loved. It describes the relationship between a people who passionately devoted themselves to God part of the time, and willfully rejected Him the rest of the time. Even though He loved them intensely, He allowed tragic consequences for their sin, because He was trying to bring them back to their senses so that they would once again follow His ways. He wanted them to be able to experience a vibrant life and genuine peace, and He knew that *obedience* to His commands was the avenue that was necessary for this to happen.

God has not changed. But today, we have the luxury of Jesus Christ, Who paid the penalty for our willful disobedience to God. He still loves humanity intensely, and He still wants a relationship with His creation more than ever (1 Peter 1:2). He displayed His overwhelming love for us when He allowed Jesus to suffer an excruciating death – one that was really more appropriate for us (Romans 5:8). As a community of Christ's followers, we are no different than the Israelites – we sometimes vacillate between loving and pleasing the Lord, to following our own path of selfishness and willful defiance.

- Are you reaping benefits from your lifestyle choices, or consequences?

<u>I didn't know that!</u>

We often view the concept of 'obedience' as drudgery. Especially when we are asked to do something we really don't want to do. We complain "People are always trying to control me!" We resist change, and we frequently refuse to bend our will to others, unless there is a benefit to us.

But did you know that biblical obedience is actually a form of worship? God is absolutely pleased when we put aside our own agenda, and instead, we deliberately choose His wisdom and direction for our lives (Isaiah 55:3-7 and Romans 8:1-14). He desperately wants us to follow His ways, because He knows that it will result in a life of contentment and satisfaction. It enables us to have healthy boundaries in our lives. And when we act in loving obedience to the Lord, it allows us the freedom to experience authentic joy.

God requires, and fully deserves, our obedience. But before we decide to 'perform' for Him in an attitude of arrogance or annoyance, we need to realize that our 'obedience' means nothing to God if we are not motivated by love. That's right! Just 'following the rules' is *not* what God had in mind for us when He laid out the plan for our lives. In fact, He <u>detests</u> our pretense of righteousness, our meaningless rituals, and our empty religion (Isaiah 1:10-20; Matthew 9:13; Matthew 12:7; and Mark 7:6-8)!

Sometimes, giving Him permission to change our desires is the hardest thing for us to allow, because it involves dying to our flesh. It's often easier to follow 'rituals' in order to try to please God, than it is to completely turn our hearts, wills, emotions, fears and hopes over to Him. But what He really wants is for our very *being* to change, with a resulting obedience that springs out of *our intense love for Him*.

Again, it's really important to understand that it's not just the 'outward' behaviors that God is concerned with. It's not the lying, drinking, cheating, cussing, and sleeping around that He is after. Obviously, He doesn't want us doing these things, because they are detrimental to our bodies, minds, and spirits. However, He is far more concerned about *our motives*, because our <u>actions</u> stem from what is in our <u>heart</u>, and this is what God really wants to change (1 Samuel 16:7). As our attitudes are transformed, our thoughts and feelings will begin to align with His. This is when our behavior will change.

- How do you react when God asks you to do something contrary to what you want to do? This can mean the time you spend helping others, sharing your money with those less fortunate, or giving up a bad habit.

He wanted us even before He made the earth

God spoke of His desire for a mutually loving relationship with mankind from the beginning of creation (Genesis 1:26-27). Incidentally, the 'Us' in this scripture is the Triune Godhead. God the Father, God the Son, and God the Holy Spirit were talking together! This is proven by the Hebrew word for 'God' used here – 'Elohim'. This word literally stands for 'plural God'. This does not mean there are *three* Gods, because God is called 'God' throughout scripture. There is only One God, but three distinct, separate Beings. It's really hard to grasp, but sometimes, God is just SO big and so supernatural that we can't always understand His ways! We just have to trust that He cannot lie in His Word (Hebrews 6:18).

Just as in the beginning, God yearns for our fellowship in exactly the same way today. But we can spoil this connection if we allow our hearts to harden. Just like the Israelites, we may go to church, say the right 'Christian' things, and even give the church our time and money. But inside, we may be far from authentically loving and worshiping God (John 12:37-40 and Hebrews 3:5-19). The Lord knows us well!

The book of Deuteronomy is a beautiful book that illustrates His love and concern for His people. He was teaching them that He wanted obedience from a heart of devotion more than anything else they could give Him. And He wants that from us now. When our hearts are fully dedicated to God, we will *want* to give Him everything we have. Then, our obedience won't be an obligation - it will be a thrill! No matter what we say, we naturally do what we ***want*** to do. As such, a sincere desire for the Lord will allow us to obey Him much more easily. It's also way more fun! It can be shown this way:

Sincere desire for the Lord = Intimate relationship with Him through the infilling of His Holy Spirit = a smoother, more peaceful, more powerful and certainly, a more joyful Christian walk. The opposite is:

> Sincere desire for our flesh and our ways = distant relationship with God and lack of the Holy Spirit's power = hardship and burnout in the Christian life = an eventual turning away from all godly things

- How would you describe your relationship with God?
- Would you say you are obedient most of the time, some of the time, or rarely?

I will **not**!

'Submission' is a word that goes hand-in-hand with obedience. We need to surrender, or submit, in order to obey a higher authority. But often, submission is also a concept that we don't really understand. The prevailing attitude in the last several decades has been 'Me first' – 'Do it if it feels good' – and 'As long as I'm not hurting anyone, I can do whatever I want'. But we have sadly distorted this beautiful picture of authentic love called 'surrender'.

We may feel smothered or defensive when we hear the word 'submit', especially in our culture today. The women's liberation movement has redefined a woman's godly position in the home, the church, and in the marketplace. And the 'mid-life crisis' issues that many men experience have led many away from the responsibilities that God intended for them to uphold. This has all contributed to a lifestyle of selfishness and independence. It's easy to see why many people are reluctant to give up control of their lives to anyone else. And we find that divorce is rampant, because couples stubbornly refuse to submit to one another (Ephesians 5:21-33).

While the literal translation for submission means 'to be in subjection under another', biblical submission is an act of our will. I'm not dismissing the fact that there are people who tragically exploit God's idea of submission by abusing their power. They purposefully lord over others by physically, mentally, emotionally, and spiritually intimidating them. Don't worry - God *will* deal with these people harshly.

But Jesus showed us a stunning example of the original intent of submission when He went to the cross on our behalf (John 10:6-18 and Philippians 2:6-8). This is the same model that we should follow when we submit to Him. Of course, we will probably never be crucified, but He does command us to 'lay down our lives' for His sake (Luke 9:23-27). This means that if we call ourselves Christians and say that we love Him, then we are to consistently make choices that put Him first in our lives. He also calls us to serve others (Matthew 20:24-28 and Galatians 5:13-21).This entails giving a generous portion of our time, talent, and money for His kingdom purposes. In this way, we will please the Lord, indeed.

- How do you react when you hear that you have to submit?

<u>Does your **life** show your **love**?</u>

Submission is also a form of worship to God. As we give our lives, plans, and possessions to Him, we are demonstrating our understanding that He really is the Owner of the universe. Anyone can SAY they love God and follow Him, but true submission *proves our love by our actions* (Matthew 12:33-35 and James 2:14-24). What we say and do is the direct result of what resides in our hearts (Matthew 15:16-19). But since our hearts are naturally deceitful and wicked (Jeremiah 17:9), we need to be cleansed by the washing of His Word and His Holy Spirit in order to live a life of obedience, one that is pleasing to Him (Romans 2:29b). It's an 'inside job' – it's not at all something we can accomplish on our own.

We have read Ephesians 5:21-23, which describes the importance of mutual submission in marriage. But the covenant of marriage is also used as a way to illustrate the relationship between God and His beloved followers. The husband is to love his wife **as** Christ loves the church and the woman is called to respect her husband. It is meant to be *mutually* submissive. If both spouses choose to lovingly yield to God first, and then to one other in the power of the Holy Spirit, then harmony and unity will result.

It's the same way when we choose to submit to God. This decision brings us tremendous blessing, because we are actively putting ourselves under His headship and protection. He made us, so He is the best one to help us plot the course for our lives. He knows what will bring us the greatest joy, and what will help us reap the most fruit for eternity. His commandments keep us from harm and bring true purpose into our lives.

Submitting to God is a fitting and healthy response to the One who loves us passionately and unconditionally. And as we live in obedience to the Lord, we will receive what we have always been looking for - peace, joy, love, hope, and purpose. Only HE can transform us in ways that we will be eternally productive and utterly satisfied.

- Can you think of a recent time when you allowed God to change your heart or mind?
- Is your attitude still reflecting this change, or have you veered back to your old ways?

The Vine and the branches

John 15 has a lot to say about being 'attached to the vine'. Only as we are actively attached to our 'Power Source' can we function in the way we were created. Just as a dead battery is of no good, when we are not 'charged' by the Holy Spirit, we are useless to God.

In this scripture, Jesus is the vine and we, as Christians, are the branches. Apart from the connection to His life-giving vine, we can bear no spiritual or eternal fruit (Matthew 7:17-20). This is the essential component to living a vital, healthy, and fruitful Christian life. We receive life and sustenance from craving the Living God and by placing our will under His authority.

It is also crucial that we are rightly and deeply related to God, the Holy Spirit (John 16:5-15). The Bible says that spiritual things are only discerned by the Spirit living within us (John 14:15-17). This means that we are unable to realize the profound truths of God's Word without the active presence of the Holy Spirit. We cannot perceive the difference between good and evil as well. And we will not be able to produce eternal fruit without His influence. This is why those that are not of the Spirit think the gospel is foolishness (1 Corinthians 2:13-16).

Although we are indwelt by God's Spirit at the moment of salvation (John 4:14), the choices we make to move towards the Lord or away from Him will govern how well the Spirit can move in us, and how well we can hear His prompting. We can literally snuff out the work of the Holy Spirit in our lives if we continue living in flagrant sin (1 Thessalonians 5:16-22). And Christians who are not filled with the Spirit lack the vitality and the holiness that is so important in winning souls to Christ (Romans 8:9-11). We need to move the old stuff out and allow God's holy things in. And the more we imitate Jesus, the more at home the Holy Spirit will be in our lives.

- How 'connected' do you feel to God?
- Do you know when the Holy Spirit is speaking to you? How can you tell?

But I'm a good person.....

Now, you might be thinking "I'm a good person. I give to charities and volunteer with the poor. I pay my taxes, and try not to hurt anyone". While you may be a really nice person, the Bible tells us that we are *all* sinners and have a selfish bent (Romans 3:10-12). And nowhere in scripture does God say that the 'nice' people will go to heaven. He makes it clear that **no one** will receive eternal life without accepting and living for Jesus Christ (John 14:6).

Only God is perfect love (1 John 4:14-17). Much of His character is outlined in 1 Corinthians 13. Read this chapter and compare yourself to it. We quickly realize none of us are living up to the absolute standard of this kind of godly love. It's a high bench-mark! And this is why we need a Savior – because we are all in the same boat when we measure ourselves against God.

Are you **sure** you are going to heaven?

Just as Jesus laid down His life and followed the plan that God had for Him while He was here on this earth , we are also given the choice to either obey God, or to live by our own standards. Notice, we see Jesus *knocking* at the door of our hearts, not bringing in the SWAT team to force our allegiance. It is our *choice* to open the door in order for Him to come in (Revelation 3:20). And Jesus was clear that it is also our decision to *continue* allowing Him reign in our lives (Matthew 13:1-23 and Revelation 3:8-13). If we refuse Him, it will be at our own peril (2 Corinthians 5:10).

So don't be deceived; the door to heaven *is* narrow (Matthew 7:13-14). Many believe they are going to heaven, but they will be dismayed at the Judgment, because they have failed to carry out the Lord's will, as evidenced by their lifestyle choices (Matthew 7:21-23 and Matthew 24:36-51).

While it is true that Jesus' shed blood gives us grace for our sins, living entirely for our own pleasure while calling ourselves by the precious name of Jesus is irreverence. We not only grieve God mightily (Ephesians 4:30), but we will experience consequences in direct proportion to what we have done or not done for Him (Matthew 25:14-46).

We have to realize that we are only given two options in this life. We can accept Jesus now and live in glory for eternity, or reject Him here and go to hell for eternity (Matthew 13:37-43 and Matthew 22:1-14). And contrary to some popular ideas, we will not have a chance to make this decision after we die (Luke 12:8-9 and Luke 13:24-30). People who refuse to acknowledge and follow Christ typically try to ignore this truth, but denying the saving power of Jesus *will* lead to eternal punishment (1 Corinthians 1:18 and Galatians 6:7-10).

- Are you absolutely sure you are going to heaven?
- Are you allowing the Spirit more and more control in your life? Or do you frequently resist His leading?

<u>Blessings can turn into curses</u>

If you are worshiping the Lord with all your heart, mind and soul, God will naturally start to pour His Spirit and blessings into your life. He is delighted when we experience His bounty, and this can be a time of great joy and contentment. But He also warns us to take particular care during this time, especially if we have come from a life of spiritual, mental, physical, or emotional bankruptcy. If we haven't developed the

Holy Spirit's gift of self control and discernment, we can spoil our newfound blessings by using them in a manner that not was intended by God.

Also, we as humans have a tendency to create idols when we have become satisfied with our lives (Deuteronomy 4:9 and Deuteronomy 4:23-24). Sometimes, we laugh at the idea of these people making wood or stone objects and then bowing down to them. But we certainly do bow down to idols - things like money, other people's opinions, sexual sin, power, prestige, sports, beauty, and unnecessary material gain. But God is adamantly against this attitude of idolatry (Exodus 20:1-6 and 1 John 2:15-17). So remember, an idol *is **anything** that takes our time and affection from God.*

We have learned that acts of service and worship must be accompanied by loving devotion from the heart, otherwise it is just **religion** ☹. We've all seen people who are living a life of religious duty. They become critical and unloving. They often do things 'in the name of the Lord' when in fact, God never ordained them in the first place. And worse yet, they turn people away from Jesus, bringing condemnation upon themselves.

The way for us to keep from becoming selfish, hard-hearted, and outwardly religious, is to train our minds to think about Jesus throughout our day. He loves it when we talk about Him and brag on Him! The Bible tells us to remind our children of who God is, and of all the wonderful things He has done for us (Deuteronomy 11:13-23). We must never forget Who redeemed us from our slavery, which is sin (Deuteronomy 6:11-13). And we are to passionately and continually praise His great name and thank Him for His glorious power. This will also keep us from a life of complaining and worrying.

Deuteronomy 8:10-11 restates this important concept: Beware that in your plenty, you don't forget the hand from Whom all your blessings flow. We can become proud of our acquisitions and our increased spirituality. What was intended for our good can easily turn into a curse if we stop giving God the credit for the goodness in our lives.

And it is important that we *keep ourselves* pure and holy so that God can use us for His purposes (1 Peter 1:13-19). It is our responsibility to let go of our past and reach for our future in Christ (Philippians 3:12-14).

- Would you say you worship God with many aspects of your life? List them.
- Or do you spend a large amount of time worrying, complaining, and criticizing?

<u>What are the benefits of obedience?</u>

When we wholeheartedly obey the Lord, He promises to provide for our every need (Deuteronomy 30:1-10). The Lord will also *delight Himself in us!* When I read that, I think of Him looking at me with eyes of absolute love. I see Him laughing and enjoying my company. I picture Him puffing up His chest because He's so proud of me, His child! That alone makes me want to please Him with everything I am and everything I have.

The Bible also says that as we live in obedience to God, we will:

display our intelligence (Deuteronomy 4:6)!

find true prosperity (Deuteronomy 4:40)

and live a <u>righteous</u> life

We will also prosper if we submit to His ways. Now, before you think "Ooh – I can get more money?", remember that God's blessings are far better than the temporary things we may think we want. They may come in the form of restored relationships, a good reputation, or a changed attitude. And what we really crave will be ours – love, joy, peace, and hope. We are also promised a close and right relationship with God, and the ultimate benefit of knowing Him. If we immerse ourselves in the Lord, we will have access to His power, His love, His comfort, and His direction.

Of course, this doesn't mean that we will never suffer again after we have chosen to love and obey God. Often, people say "Well, I became a Christian, but I still have so many problems". The truth is, we will have troubles in this life regardless if we follow Christ or not. And if we are genuinely following Him in obedience, we may experience a whole new set of trials in our lives! The Lord spoke frequently about the probability of His followers being persecuted in this world (Matthew 5:10-12; 5:44; John 15:18-25 and 16:33). But if we patiently endure the pruning that God allows for our benefit, we will reap a harvest of strength, character, and hope that would have never been possible without the trials (Romans 5:1-5).

The fact is, Jesus does not promise a life of 'happiness'. But He does promise that we will receive joy if we love and follow Him with all of our might (John 15:10-11). Besides, happiness is transient – it is here today, and gone tomorrow. But real joy that is given to us by the Holy Spirit lies deep within our souls and cannot be easily shaken (Romans 15:13 and 1 Peter 1:8-9).

Another amazing truth is that we actually *become* holy when we obey God (Deuteronomy 7:6 and 1 Peter 1:22). When we trust in His wisdom, we will experience a new vitality in our lives, and we will produce a harvest of peace and righteousness (James 3:17-18). Deuteronomy 30 is a whole chapter telling us about the benefits of returning to the Lord. When He is our life, then we have everything! But if we are living without Him, then our spirit is dead. We are missing a huge portion of who we really are.

Uh Oh!

Now that we have seen some of the benefits of obedience, let's see what happens when we choose *not* to obey.

Deuteronomy 28 is a chapter that lists 14 blessings that result from obedience, and 68 curses for disobedience! Since there are more than twice the consequences for *not* obeying, it is important to find out what disobedience really is. We see that it is:

1. rejecting God's love,
2. rebelling against His authority,
3. ignoring His commands for right living,
4. willfully breaking your relationship with Him,
5. and not living out what you have confessed about your faith in Him.

Disobedience also includes the hardening of your heart (through rejecting God's ways), an ungrateful attitude towards the things that God has done for you, and an uncaring spirit towards other people, especially those in the household of God.

This heart condition displays some level of spiritual death.

Are you dead?

Revelation 3:1 speaks about having a 'reputation of being alive' but actually being spiritually dead. If this is true in our lives, we may be giving the world and our church the 'picture of health' on the outside, but the Spirit is no longer controlling us. Too many Christians live in this 'deathly' state. They may even leave the faith for this very reason- thinking that Christianity didn't really 'deliver' for them. If they continue on this road, they will eventually cease to even care that they are spiritually corrupt.

The reality is - we are not meant to live our lives apart from the Spirit of God. He is the One that initially gave us life (Genesis 2:7)! He is the One who rebirths the new life in our spirits. And He is the only One who can empower us and guide us into living a righteous life.

If we become more concerned with trying to be religious or trying to impress others than with pleasing God, then we are controlling the 'outside' of our lives, but allowing the inside to rot. We will miss God even though we are actually deceived into thinking that we are worshiping Him! Jesus spoke of this when He was rebuking the Pharisees, the group of religious leaders in His time. Outwardly, they were very devout, but inside, they were full of pride, greed, and selfishness. Jesus said that they were like white washed tombs – beautiful on the outside but definitely DEAD on the inside (Matthew 23:23-28).

- How 'alive' do you think you are for Jesus? For example, when was the last time you shared Him with someone? Have you ever led anyone to salvation in Christ?

How can I stay spiritually alive?

Jesus reminds us to turn back to the things we did when we first fell in love with Him (Revelation 2:1-5). Start at His Cross. What did Jesus do for you there? Remember how excited you were to find Him when you first got saved? Remember how deeply grateful you felt about His blood sacrifice on your behalf? That your sins were forgiven and you were cleansed and free? Remember how much energy you had to read His Word, to witness, and to pray? When we relive the time when we first fell in love with Him, we realize anew all He has done for us. As we begin to praise Him, our hearts will soften and we will develop a new gratitude for the things of the Lord.

If you are in this scary place, you should make an immediate *choice* to turn your thoughts back to Jesus. Begin thanking Him for every single little thing in your life. When thoughts of worry and frustration crowd your mind, refocus your mind on Jesus and think of all the ways He makes each day better for you. Make **Him** your 'default' thought!

Deuteronomy 8:19-20 says that we will be destroyed if we refuse to live God's way! If we choose to remain in rebellion, we are the ones to lose. Remember, living part of your life for God and another part of your life for any other 'god' is not only disobedience, it is idolatry. He wants our *total* allegiance. He adores you! And He desires your intimate friendship.

The Bible warns us that we are not immune from the curses of disobedience. Again, thinking we are safe even though we are continuing to walk in our own stubborn way is spiritual death (Deuteronomy 29:19-21). While He IS love, and He showed amazing grace at the Cross, part of His character is also justice. Because of this, He cannot turn away from His own holiness. He must demand payment for disobedience. If we refuse the price that Jesus already paid, then we have to pay our own way. And our own payment is but filthy rags – it will **never** be close enough to pay our debt.

- Are you willing to change and step out of your comfort zone so that your life actually *reflects* Jesus?

<u>But I'm so tired....</u>

Perhaps you are in a valley or wilderness experience right now. Obeying God may be the last thing you feel like doing. There will be times in our walk when we feel no energy or passion for God. We may feel as if He has abandoned us. Or, we might be in a place where we are so exhausted, we don't even have the energy to respond to what

God is asking of us. But this is the *perfect* time to go back to the basics in our relationship with the Lord. He alone can give us the strength, energy, and focus to live a life of overcoming victory!

The problem is that many times, we try to live for Jesus in our own strength. This is when we get tired of trying to do things Gods way. We try to move ahead of His schedule, thinking that He's just not working fast enough. So we try to take over, and bulldoze our way through situations that were meant to be a time of waiting and testing to develop our character.

Maybe you're thinking "I do so many things for God, and I still feel so empty". But if this is true, we need to once again check our motives. *Why* are we doing 'so much for God'? The truth is, if we feel burned out while serving Him, then we are not living in His power (2 Corinthians 4:7 and 13:3-4)! Don't worry - we are never going to be absolutely obedient. This is precisely why Christ came to take our place. We deserve God's wrath, but He knew we didn't have the strength to overcome our natural tendencies. But Jesus' death and resurrection *gave* us the very power we need to serve Him and others, and to have victory over sin!

Be grateful! Continue thanking Him for your health, your home, your children, your job, the provision of food, warmth, and clothing. Thank Him for your relationships. As we do this, we take our eyes off of our troubles and focus on how much we REALLY have! Remind yourself of His sacrifice for you every day. And continue to ask the Holy Spirit to breathe HIS life into yours.

- Are you feeling energized by the Holy Spirit in your life right now?
- Or do you feel like all you're doing is just trying to get by, and you'll get to Him when you finally have a little extra time?

So, how can I learn to obey?

God instructs us to walk in His ways by revering Him, praising Him, and thanking Him (Ephesians 5:15-20). We are to guard against our natural tendency towards pride. We are never to forget what He has done for us (Deuteronomy 8:6, 14, and 15). We are to destroy our old lives (Deuteronomy 12:1-9), and instead, cling to the Lord (Deuteronomy 13:3-4)!

If we consistently meditate on His Word and His character, we *will* be able to live triumphantly. We are to live each day by the Truth He has laid out for us in scripture. And if we incline our ear to His every breath and listen to what His Holy Spirit frequently reveals to us, we will be moved by God Himself!

It's simple, but not always easy! However, laying down your life to Him in submission will be much less difficult if you make lifestyle choices to stay in His presence.

God's will for our lives

Many people ask "What is the Lord's will for my life?" We see the answers from the following scriptures. He wants us to:

fear Him (this means reverence, respect, and awe; not to be afraid),
live according to his Word,
imitate Him
love him,
worship Him with all of our heart and soul,
obey his commands (Deuteronomy 10:12-21)
do what is right
love mercy
and to walk humbly with Him (Micah 6:8).

So often, we try to 'measure up' or attempt to gain favor with God by what we *do*. Stop there! Ask Him to fill you with *His* power. It's <u>His</u> job to change our hearts, minds and attitudes so that our behavior reflects that of Jesus! Philippians 2:13 says that God works in us, *giving us the desire to obey Him and the power to do what pleases Him*. He's got us covered! Our job is to get closer to Him day by day.

We've read that the best way to please the Lord is to love Him with all of our hearts, souls, and strength (Deuteronomy 6:4-6). But we can deepen this love even more by talking with Him frequently in prayer, and by reading His Word often. We develop godliness by spending time alone in reflection and self-examination, and by spending quality time with other Christians who exhibit the fruit of God's Spirit (Galatians 5:22-23). As in any relationship, the amount of effort we put forth has a direct influence on the level of intimacy we experience. We literally become transformed as we spend time with the Lord (Romans 12:2), and obedience becomes the **fruit** of our efforts (Colossians 1:9-10).

Are you frustrated from trying to please God? Do you feel like you're drying up in the spiritual desert? Then worship Jesus passionately by investing your time, energy, emotions, talents, and thoughts into your relationship with Him and His kingdom. Jesus IS the living water for our souls. You will experience untold blessings just by worshiping Him! When we fix our minds on what is good and lovely and worthy, we take our minds off of ourselves and we become more like Jesus (Philippians 4:4-8). God is there, just waiting to help you through your life.

'Obedience is the key to the Father's heart'

REFLECTION

1. What is obedience?

2. Do you fear submitting your life to God in order to obey Him?

3. What are some of the benefits of obeying Him?

4. What are some negative consequences we might experience by disobeying Him?

5. What are some things we can do if we feel dry or empty in our spiritual walk?

6. What are two things that we can do in order to make our obedience much easier to accomplish?

7. Why does God want us to obey Him?

8. What are your motives for serving and obeying God? (Be completely honest. If you are frustrated in your life with Christ, this will help you to determine why)

Some answers might be: "I want to look good", "I want to gain favor with Him", "I want to feel part of my church family", or "I want to get more brownie points so He will love me more".

NOTES

SELF-ESTEEM

'Self esteem' has been a common buzzword in the last couple of decades. It's a concept that is a bit hard to define. But we do know that some people are so absorbed with their 'low self esteem', they are literally debilitated by their feelings of inadequacy. Others believe that it's something only neurotic women obsess about. And still others believe that 'working on' one's self esteem is just a bunch of nonsense.

The truth is that low self esteem affects both men and women, in every stratosphere of life. Whether we are rich or poor, beautiful or ugly, old or young, educated or ignorant, we have all experienced a time when we have suffered from feelings of inferiority.

There are thousands of books out there telling us how to feel better about ourselves. And counseling is a multi-million dollar business. But people don't really seem to be getting any better! Indeed, there are more people in this society that are addicted, disordered, and suicidal than almost any other time in history – and it's often because they lack genuine, healthy self esteem.

<u>What *is* self-esteem?</u>

The English word for 'esteem' means 'to value, admire, respect, regard, and to prize'. Thus, '*self* esteem' is seeing ourselves in a positive light. God created us to feel confident about ourselves, but He designed us to live in a mutual relationship with Him in order for this to be realized in the healthiest way possible.

In order to overcome our feelings of inadequacy, we need to get rid of our old mindsets. It is essential to combat the lies we believe about ourselves. This is done by learning the Truth about who we really are.

Why do I think so poorly of myself?

Part of the reason why people suffer from low self-esteem is related to the method by which they measure their thoughts, attitudes, and conduct. We live in a society where we are bombarded by television, radio, and billboards that promise happiness, beauty, and long life, if only we do or buy what they are selling. We have been brain-washed by psychologists and sociologists to believe that 'only the fittest survive'. And many people spend huge amounts of time, energy, and money trying to maintain a false pretense that they have their lives 'together'.

To add to these impossible demands for perfection, women are expected to work, while maintaining a home, staying gorgeous, keeping a satisfied husband, and having wonderful children. Men are expected to work and to fulfill their tender, fatherly sides, and to be ideal husbands so their wives won't wander. We have come to a point where we seem to think that if we're not constantly performing, and we aren't meeting everyone's demands at all times, that we are complete failures. And to top it off, we frequently worry that we are going to lose whatever we have.

But God never intended for us to 'be all that' every moment of every day. If we try to keep up this pretentious way of living, we will end up feeling less significant than ever. None of us can keep up this unrealistic treadmill of accomplishment.

God is just waiting for us to ask for His help, so that we won't have to carry our burdens alone (1 Peter 5:7). Judging ourselves by others' standards only brings frustration and disappointment in the long run, because people and fads change daily. So, if we're spending our days frantically trying to compete, we will fail in some aspect of our spiritual, mental, emotional, or physical lives.

- What are some ways that you measure yourself against others?
- Do you feel better after you finish your comparison?

<u>What is *God's* opinion of me?</u>

The Bible tells us that we were fashioned by God's own hands. We were also individually made (Psalm 139:13-16). This means that He was there, creating every single one of our cells in our mother's womb. He chose to form you exactly the way He wanted you. Thus, we are of immeasurable worth to Him! And we are so valuable to God that He purchased us from our slavery to sin with a very costly, precious price – the life of His Son, Jesus. This was the ultimate demonstration of His absolute love for us (1 Peter 1:16-19).

When we hate ourselves, put ourselves down, or feel worthless, we are, in fact, criticizing and degrading the most beautiful and important of all of God's creation! When we think we're not good enough, we are actually believing the biggest lie of all. Genesis 1:31 says that were created excellently in every way – and that God is pleased with how He made us! Jesus adores us, and *this love* is the foundation that we need to build our confidence on.

- What are some things you say to yourself on a daily basis?
  - Maybe it's "I can do this"; or "I'm never going to make it"; or "I don't have to listen to them – I've got it all figured out".
- Begin listening to your 'self-talk' and you may be surprised at what you hear.

I wish I was.....

Humans have the tendency to compare themselves with others. The problem with doing this is that we usually end up feeling either proud or inferior. When pride is the root, we may search for ways to make ourselves look better by putting others down. We feel puffed up when we find fault in others. However, the Bible says that God hates pride (Proverbs 8:13), so it's clear that this is not a healthy attitude. Ironically, even if you feel terrible about yourself, pride may be the culprit. This is because self-absorption *is* the basis of pride – it's really positioning *yourself* at the center of the universe, instead of the One Who should be there – God alone.

And if inferiority has a grip on us, we find that we constantly compare ourselves with others. We lament the fact that we will never have 'those looks' or 'that talent' or 'those things' or 'that money', and we feel like we are not good enough.

But since we are made in the image of the Triune Godhead (Genesis 1:26), and Jesus Christ shed His own blood for our sakes (Revelation 1:5), we **must choose** to believe the truth - that we are extremely special and important to Him.

In essence, neither pride nor inferiority are godly qualities. And when we insist on evaluating ourselves according to the worlds' opinions instead of Gods', then we find the core of our low self esteem.

- What are some ways that you wish you were different?
- In what ways do you compare yourself with others? (wishing you had their money, looks, fame, talent, things, family, etc).....
- Do you think that your money, looks, talent, kids, possessions, or your job are what make you worthy?

What's the big deal?

Another problem we run into when we compare ourselves to others, is that we either sink into self-pity, or we try to become *better* than them. This if folly! What we tend to forget is that they are just *people!* Humans are all basically the same – we all need love, food, clothing, shelter, and companionship. We all have fears, hopes, and preferences. If fact, you have certain gifts that the person you're measuring yourself against does not. And certainly, no one is perfect!

We also miss out on the potential enjoyment of others, because we're so busy critiquing their lives. When we are envious of them, or looking down our nose at them, we are ignoring the fact that they have problems, too. They have good and bad character traits, just like all of us. But if we feel good about ourselves, and we allow them to be who they are without judging them, we may find we like this extraordinary person and we might even find a new friend.

Additionally, when we use external things like money, fame, physical strength, or beauty to identify ourselves, we find that these conditions can change. This world is so fragile! We are foolish to build our identity on these temporary things, because everything we see right now will eventually wither and die (1 Peter 1:24).

But with God.....

You see, when we measure ourselves with God's yardstick, we are measured *individually*. The changes that God wants to make in us are so that we can grow into the unique person that He has designed us to be. He designed us so that we can become more like Jesus, not so we can become more like other people!

When our identity is grounded in the Lord and what *He* thinks of us, our lives will become more consistent and secure, because God is a foundation that will never change! And when we begin to realize the truth that we are **already** the 'apple of God's eye', we can stop striving to be 'worthy' enough (Ephesians 1:3-8).

Instead, we can begin to use our energy to change our old thoughts (Romans 12:2). As we focus more and more on the Lord, our hearts will change, and we'll have a renewed sense of vitality. And this new lifestyle will translate into helping others, instead of selfishly living only for ourselves.

When we believe what God says about us in His Word, it will give us the stability we need in order to mature as Christians. We need to spend our time concentrating on the eternal truths of His kingdom, not staring at our bellybuttons!

- Have you ever measured yourself against God's standards?
- Do you know what His Word says about you?
- Have you ever accepted Jesus Christ into your heart?

<u>I'm in control!</u>

Another problem we have that can lead to low self worth is believing that we are the only ones completely in charge of our lives. Sometimes, we feel like we're the only ones that are capable of running the show. But in reality, this attitude creates fear, uneasiness and uncertainty, because we were never intended to live apart from God. He is the ruler of the universe, and when we try to usurp His power by insisting on managing our lives without Him, we are setting ourselves up for emptiness and failure.

The Bible says that only as we humble ourselves under the mighty hand of God will we be elevated (1 Peter 5:6). God knew we would have difficulty submitting to Him, so right after the instruction to humble ourselves, He immediately tells us to turn our insecurities over to Him!

He also knew that depending only on ourselves would result in unhealthy feelings, thoughts, and behaviors. When we make our life's decisions by human wisdom alone, we lack the spiritual discernment that comes from having a relationship with the Lord. It's like asking instructions about how to maneuver a boat from someone who has never sailed before.

God is the **only** expert on human behavior. Thus, *He* is the only One whose opinion really matters. When we forget or ignore this important concept, we fail to rely on the One who has the power to transform our lives. We rob ourselves of the only Person who has the power and the desire to help us to live up to our true potential (Philippians 2:13). In reality, the only way we really 'make it' in this life is when *God* has made us fit for His kingdom.

- In which areas of your life do you feel you have absolute control?
- Do you feel you <u>must</u> have this control?
- What would happen if you turned this struggle with control over to God?

<u>One more thing....</u>

There is still another issue we may experience that has the power to destroy our self worth: worry. People spend an extraordinary amount of time thinking about 'what if's'. But really - most of what we worry about *never* comes to pass. This is why Jesus tells us simply "Do not worry!" (Matthew 6:25-34). God is big enough to fix our mistakes, to help us out of the miry clay, and to turn what was meant for our harm into good (Genesis 50:20). He is our Provider, our Sustainer, our Safety, our Rescuer, and our Redeemer. What we need to do is start *training our minds* to believe that no matter what, God WILL take care of us. Peace comes when we *fix* our thoughts on Him (Isaiah 26:3-4).

Interestingly, even persecuted Christians around the world who have no earthly status, looks or possessions to speak of, declare that Jesus has given them all they need to succeed! This is because they realize that *true* worth, success, and overcoming power arise from knowing Jesus intimately and intensely, and by living out the Word of God. They risk their very lives to display the fact that they love the Lord with all of their hearts, minds, and souls. Believe it or not, *that* is the secret to living a victorious Christian life.

- Think about the last situation you worried about:

  -Did you ask God to help you through your situation?

  -Did you *allow* Him to take control of the things that you had no power over?

  -Did you take responsibility for the things you did have control over?

  -How did the situation turn out?

<u>God is my Daddy!</u>

We are God's children! In fact, the Bible uses the term 'Abba', which translates to our English word for 'Daddy'. It is used to illustrate the act of a child calling upon their father with love, tenderness, and trust. We as Christians have heard that 'we are His children' so much, we sometimes fail to realize its significance.

We often have the tendency to think of ourselves as the 'adults' in our relationship with the Lord. Therefore, our attitude is "I'll ask God for His help when I *really* need it". But this mindset defeats the intention He has for His beloved creation. He calls us 'children' because He wants us to think of Him as the One whom we can run to even when we get the smallest scrape on our knees!

Even if we had terrible parents growing up, we can still receive the attention and affection that we may have missed from our earthly father. We can truly be healed from every sort of neglect or abuse that we have experienced. And even if we were raised in a good family, there are probably things we wish were different. No matter the circumstances, we find *everything* our heart desires when we love and trust our Father in heaven.

- Do you believe that you are beloved by God?
- If not, would you be willing to pray to Him so that you can begin a relationship?

<u>We're adopted!</u>

Another biblical concept that explains our significance to God is that Christians are 'adopted' into God's family (Romans 8:15). This may not sound very important- until we realize what this meant in biblical times. It's a very different situation from what we think of when we hear the word 'adopted' today.

In the New Testament times, Roman families would adopt children into their homes. The adopted child was given every single privilege that the biological child had. They were recipients and heirs to everything the family owned. It was as if they had been actually born to the parents.

And this is exactly the same picture as the standing we have in Christ. We are adopted into the bloodline, and as such, we *are* 'biological' children of God. We will receive everything Jesus has, in heaven and on earth, as our inheritance (Ephesians 2:6; 3:6 and 1 Peter 1:3-4).

Sometimes, we forget that we have a divine reason for being here. The Bible says that God will *crown us with glory and honor* (Romans 8:16-17; 2 Thessalonians 2:13-14 and 1 Peter 1:6-7). We don't seem to understand the truth that as authentic Christians, God will eventually give us authority over all things (Hebrews 2:6-8)! In fact, someday we will even judge the world and the angels (1 Corinthians 6:2-3).

This relates to our self esteem, because we are literally *royalty*! Jesus is the King, *and* the Prince of Peace (Revelation 17:14; Revelation 19:16, and Isaiah 9:6). And we are His beloved family! Sometimes as Christians, we act like we are destitute. We often go through life believing that this is all there is, and it's up to us to make our lives successful. But God wants us to rely completely on Him, instead!

Additionally, we often think of this world as the only reality there is. We act as if it's the only thing that really matters. We have already read that this earth and everything in it is dying, decaying, and passing away. But our lives in Christ will last for eternity (1 Peter 1:23). God makes it clear that there are more things unseen than seen – and we are not to place our faith in temporary things we can see, touch, taste, and smell (Romans 1:20; 2 Corinthians 4:16-18 and Hebrews 11:3). It is only as we believe God at His Word, will we gain new insight into eternity. Then, we will begin to value ourselves the way He does.

THESE truths are what we need to build our worth and our self-esteem upon. It is our *responsibility* to focus our thoughts and train our minds on His Word, which is perfect and absolutely true. And we are to build the foundation of our lives upon this certainty (Matthew 7:21-27).

- Do you see yourself as a person with little hope, and nothing to offer? Or do you see yourself as a child in the King's bloodline?

Hooray! We're *grafted*, too ☺

What the heck does 'grafted' mean? Well, this is another way that the Bible explains just how much God loves us. First of all, we see in the Old Testament that He chose the Hebrew nation as His beloved people. He demonstrated His passion for them by miraculously setting them free from their slavery in Egypt (Leviticus 26:12-13). This is a significant concept, because much later, Jesus came to set us free from our bondage to sin.

Jesus also demonstrated His love for *us* by dying a criminal's death in our place. And He was resurrected to show His power over sin and the grave, so that we, too, would have the ability to overcome our flesh and this world.

The Jewish people were referred to as the 'original tree', because they were God's first loved people. And we as Christians are the 'grafted branches' into the original tree. *Grafting* is when you cut a branch off of one tree in order to place it into the trunk of another tree. In time, it 'fuses' together and becomes part of the other tree. When it is fully grafted, it looks as if it had been there all along.

This is the picture of Christ's followers. God loved us and wanted us so much, that He went to great lengths to 'graft' us into the original family that He had chosen. Jesus' death and resurrection made this possible. Now, both Jews who believe in Christ, and non-Jews who are Christians are all part of God's family (Romans 11:13-24). Understanding this should help us to realize how important we really are to Him.

Jesus is the foundation of genuine self esteem

One of the most harmful aspects about trying to live according to the worlds' measuring stick is that it can affect our relationship with God. When we are continually in 'comparison mode', this attitude affects our union with Him. Many people won't set foot in a church because they think they have to 'have it all together' before they can have fellowship with the Lord. Even as Christians, we sometimes fear that we do not measure up to God's demands. And when we feel unworthy, we usually have trouble coming into His presence. But with Jesus, we don't have to measure up! He went to the cross so that we *could* measure up!

The truth is that 'while we were *still* sinners, Christ died for us' (Romans 5:8). He showered us with love when we didn't deserve it in the least. While God *does* expect us to put off our old lives and exchange it for our new identity in Him, we need to realize that regardless of what we *do*, His love for us will always be the same (Romans 8:31-39).

And His love for us is an example of how we should love ourselves. We need to realize that we are valuable, precious, and loved, no matter what. We can relax, because our worth in God's eyes is not measured by our performance. His love *never* changes, and we are *always* accepted by Him. And <u>this is how we need to treat ourselves</u>. Although we need to remain humble because our source for life is the Lord and not ourselves, we *can and should* live life confidently, because the King of the Universe desires our company!

We are made in God's image, which means we were created to reflect His character. This alone can provide a solid basis for self-worth. When we know where we began, why we are here, how loved we really are, what our purpose is, and where we are going for eternity, we can stop trying to be good enough. We can quit comparing ourselves to others, because our self-worth is based on the fact that Almighty God loves us and wants us. And as healthy, biblical, self-love develops, we will steadily lose our insecurities, self-hatred, shame and guilt.

The truth is, we are absolutely *wonderful*, not because of what we have done or not done, but because we are the object of God's affection! His requirements are that we accept Jesus Christ as our payment for sin. We need to believe that He was raised from the dead, and He now lives eternally in heaven. And we are to love the Lord with all of our hearts, souls, and strength, by thinking of Him often and serving Him with all that we have (Deuteronomy 6:4-9).

Other people evaluate us by what we wear, how much we have, how we perform, what we achieve, and how we look. But God cares for us despite our shortcomings, because He created us for the very purpose of being in relationship with us. Therefore, knowing the *character of God* is really the basis of our self worth.

- Do you think of yourself as valuable and confident, or unworthy and incapable?
- Are you *willing* to believe that you are extremely important and destined for greatness in His kingdom because of God's opinion of you?

<u>The Eternal Triune God</u>

There are several eternal truths that are essential for us to accept if we are to overcome this feeling of low self esteem. First of all, we need to focus on the fact that God alone is perfect. Secondly, that Jesus Christ is the *exact* representation of God (Colossians 1:15-20). This is important, because when we place our faith in Him, He knows how to perfectly handle our lives.

Jesus is not just a 'good teacher' or a 'popular prophet', as some religions believe. We find in John 1:1-5 that one of Jesus' names is 'the Word' and He has lived forever. This proves His divine nature, because in the Jewish mind, 'the Word' meant 'the Agent of Creation'. Since only God has the power to create something out of nothing, we understand that Jesus is also God. He was there at the formation of the universe, which would have only been possible if He was God.

Thirdly, the Holy Spirit is the third Person of this Godhead. He has the power to change our hearts, convict us of sin, comfort us during extreme hardship, and give us profound understanding of God's mind, which only God can do! (John 16:5-15; Romans 8:5-14).

And lastly, we see that the Bible is also called 'the Word'. It is eternal, as well (Isaiah 40:8). It is also alive, and it has the power to expose our innermost thoughts and desires, examine our hearts, determine our errors, and lead us into all Truth (Hebrews 4:12 and 2 Timothy 3:16). While the Bible was written by men, it is not just a collection of stories from their own wisdom. Contrary to what some believe about the Bible, the words were inspired (God-breathed). And logically, only God could have written a Book that supernaturally changes the inner workings of the human heart. But the only way to truly experience this truth is to believe in Jesus for yourself.

Now, to believe and obey!

Reading the Word of God and doing what it says is the only way our thoughts and feelings are going to be turned around so that we can understand spiritual truths and have the mind of Christ (1 Corinthians 2:13-16). Before I became a Christian, I felt absolutely worthless; I didn't even want to live. And when I began reading the Bible, it was extremely difficult for me to accept what it said. This was because I had accepted so many lies about myself, I actually thought I was believing a lie when I tried to believe the Bible! I just couldn't comprehend that God Himself would find *me* worthy enough to love.

But as I continued to read and absorb His Word, the Holy Spirit started transforming my thoughts, and I began to believe the truth about myself. I started to *trust* what GOD said about me in His Word.

Today, I feel confident and loved, and I am absolutely assured that God will equip me with whatever I need in order to carry out His plans and desires. Make no mistake

– saturating our minds with God's thoughts and opinions takes work, but it is essential if we want to feel positive and worthy in our lives.

- How much time do you spend in the Word of God? Praying? Meditating?

God's love is the BASIS for our self-esteem

Below are some extremely valuable scriptures that relate to our self worth. You can print them and read them often. Memorize them so you have ammunition against your old thoughts and the devil's attacks when you feel insecure or unworthy. We need to be immersed in His Word!

1 John 4:10, 19	God loved us first
Psalm 139:1-18	He loves us intensely
Ephesians 1:4	He had us in His plan before He made the earth
Ephesians 1:11	We are united with Christ
	We have received an inheritance from God
	God chose us in advance
Ephesians 2: 1-6	We are seated in the heavenly realms with Jesus
Ephesians 2:10	We are God's masterpiece, created for a very specific purpose in His plans
Romans 8:17	We are joint heirs with Jesus Christ (we'll inherit everything He has)
Romans 8:28	Even in our trials and suffering, He makes everything work out for our good, according to *His* plans and purpose
Hebrews 13:8	He never changes, so we can confidently place our trust in Him
Hebrews 6: 18	He cannot lie, so His promises to us for strength, purpose, and eternal life are absolutely trustworthy and dependable

Psalm 56:8	He saves our tears in a bottle
Psalm 116:1-2	He bends down and listens to us, which means we are extremely important to Him
	He hears every single prayer we utter
Psalm 121	He does not tire or sleep, so no matter what time of day we need Him, He is awake and attentive to our needs, requests, and praises
	He HIMSELF watches over us!! This means that the God of the Universe is the *very One* keeping an eye on us every second of every day
Isaiah 41:10	Don't be afraid or discouraged – God will help you and strengthen you. *He will hold you in His victorious right hand!*
Isaiah 43:1	He has called you by name (this is intensely personal)

How can we read these scriptures and not believe that we are cared for and loved – and worthy of God's attention?

He created us.

He adores us.

He desires us.

He wants to be in relationship with us.

He has a master plan for our lives.

We are the highlight of His creation!!

This is the awesome God we serve. When we understand this deep, abiding, eternal, never-changing love, we will begin to experience plenty of healthy self-esteem. I know this from experience! When we really *know* who we are, and we put our entire lives under the watchful eye of our loving God, it will result in a life of humble thankfulness and service to our Creator, which is what we were created to be and do from the moment of conception.

So, we see that the world is temporary, changing, and fading. But God the Father, God the Son, God the Holy Spirit, and the written Word of God are eternally alive and astoundingly powerful. Therefore, these are the only standards that we should be measuring ourselves against, because they will never fade or change (Hebrews 13:8). Living God's way brings healthy self-love, stability, and hope for the future.

If He is *this* devoted to us, we must begin to believe that we *are* worthy of His attention and love! Our real identity and self worth is IN CHRIST! We no longer need to feel afraid or inferior, because when we place our trust in Him, our lives will be built, not on the whims of society or the deceptive lies we have believed, but on the solid foundation of God's Truth!

* * * * * *

Remember, this world is passing. Try to look at every day and every situation in the light of eternity. When my life is done, is what I'm worrying about today going to matter? The answer will most likely be 'no'. We literally waste our lives if all we do is focus on our frailties, fears, and insecurities. But a life of confidence in Christ will produce eternal fruit, as well as joy, peace, and hope. What will matter when you see Jesus face-to-face is how well you loved Him, how well you served Him by reflecting Him to this lost world, and how well you brought others to heaven with you.

That is the stuff that will last *forever.*

REFLECTION

1. What do we have to do in order to have God love us?

2. What are some horrible things we do that can change God's love for us? (The answer is *nothing!* While we can disappoint God, alienate Him, and grieve Him, His **love** for us will not change *no matter what* we do).

3. How does His love change our love for ourselves?

4. If God loves us no matter what, does that mean we can do whatever we want and still be in relationship with Him?

5. What should we measure our self-worth/self-esteem against?

6. What are some things that we actually DO measure ourselves against? Why is this so dangerous?

7. In our relationship with Jesus, why is it essential to understand that our identity (which is our position in life, our self-worth, and our self-evaluation) is completely grounded in Him?

8. How can we make this understanding real and vital in our lives?

NOTES

REPENTANCE

Where are you in life right now? Are you in a place where you feel sad, afraid, mean, frustrated, or hopeless? Are you experiencing anger, bitterness, loneliness, emptiness, or wishing that your life was more fulfilling? Do you wish that you felt better about yourself? Maybe you wonder if your life should have more purpose than just getting up for work, taking care of the family, and buying stuff.

How about your spiritual life? Are you experiencing a deeply intense relationship with Jesus? Or are you at the opposite end, running life by your own made-up rules? Are you sitting on the fence in regards to your faith – not really hot or cold? Or maybe you're a Christian, but you feel guilty because your life looks nothing like the one Jesus talks about.

Well, take heart! Your misery may be the very thing God will use to change your life! The good news is, *no matter where you are or what you have done, Jesus is looking for you and wants to have an intimate relationship with you.* And repentance is exactly the place to start that relationship.

- Stop here and read through each of the emotions listed in the first paragraph above.

- Think about each one and write down a short sentence about how it is affecting you in your life right now.

What does *repentance* have to do with me?

Repentance is actually a military term which means to turn 180 degrees from the direction you are headed. In biblical, spiritual terms, it means to turn from our old lives, and purposefully head in the direction that Jesus wants us to go (Matthew 4:17 and Acts 20:21). Repentance also means 'reformation after guilt' or 'reversal of one's decision'. Basically, it means admitting that our ways are not right, and deciding that CHANGE needs to take place so that our lives line up with God's ways. The only pre-requisite to repentance is a soft heart that is *truly* sorry for sin, and the willingness to change (Psalm 38:18).

Repentance is the method by which we initially come to know God. It's also an ongoing lifestyle choice, because repentance should follow our sinful actions. The more we bend our will to the Savior, the more like Him we will become. And sharing our shortcomings and failures with God is an essential component to growing, and living a rewarding Christian life.

There are two elements to repentance, which are 'confession' and 'change'. Confession is also comprised of two parts, which includes 'voicing our sin', and then 'allowing God to mold our hearts and minds into His likeness'. Confession means that God wants us to use our words to define what it is we have done wrong. This makes our sin more real to us, because when we only 'think' of our offense, we have a lot more trouble sorting out our feelings, and it's also a lot easier to keep our secrets hidden.

Even more importantly, the Bible says that without confession, God does not listen to our prayers (Psalm 66:16-20). And if we have ill feelings with someone, we are to reconcile with them before we offer the sacrifice of worship to the Lord (Matthew

5:23-24). Clearly, God wants us to be free of anger, guilt and resentment, because He knows it poisons our relationships with others and with Him. Remember, the literal word for repentance means 'turning around', which implies that our minds, emotions, and actions play a major part in our decision to change.

Oh no, not *God!*

Many people run from the whole idea of having a relationship with God. They spend their whole lives trying *everything* possible to be 'happy', but they foolishly and purposefully resist the ONE person that can really bring them deep and lasting joy (Psalm 14:1)! Oftentimes, this is because they are unwilling to 'give up' ungodly behaviors in their lives. Or, they think that being a Christian will be boring, or that they will be labeled 'weird' or 'intolerant'. So they end up rejecting God and His people at all costs.

Sadly, some of these very people have been raised in 'religious' homes, and the 'Christian' adults they watched while growing up showed little of the love of Christ. Many times, their experiences of their families' hypocrisies have turned them away from Jesus and the Christian faith altogether. Or, they may decide to follow other religions or human rituals of relating to God.

And let's not forget those who have suffered abuse in their families, and they think that God has failed them. They may have wondered "If God is real, why would He have allowed that to happen to me?" They feel abandoned by the Lord, and they think He doesn't really care about them. Mistakenly, they assume that He wouldn't want them in their sinful state, anyways. And tragically, there are those that have come to actually hate God, and they have closed their hearts and minds to Him like a steel trap.

But ironically, we often find that our search for God begins when we feel dissatisfied, empty, sorrowful, or out of control in our lives. Something is telling us there is more to life, and we know deep down that we are missing whatever it is.

Why do I need to repent?

You might be wondering what it is that is so important about repentance. After all, if God knows everything, then why do I have to TELL Him my sins all the time? And why do I have to keep changing? Doesn't He love me just the way I am?

Well, just like opening a wound to release the infection inside, confession and repentance gets rid of the grime inside. We *all* have grime inside of us! And repentance is often the only thing that will bring spiritual, mental, emotional, and sometimes, even physical healing (James 5:16). On the other hand, if we harbor our sins, or we continue to sin without shame, we allow that stench to infect us (Psalm 38:5). The end result is a harvest of unhealthy living, which may result in increased guilt, anger, pride, jealousy, depression, ungratefulness, and fear. We don't have to look far to see the rage, lust, and immorality that are out of control in our world. These behaviors are often directly related to unconfessed and unrepented sin, which also leads to repressed guilt.

Disobedience comes in many forms. Obviously, it is any kind of rebellion against God's authority. But James 4:17 describes another type of sin: "It is sin to know what you ought to do, and then not do it". When we continually ignore God, or refuse to repent and change the things we know He is asking us to change, our hearts become inflexible, and our consciences' become dull.

People misunderstand the true meaning of repentance. All too often, they believe they are too good to bow their knee to anyone. Perhaps they think of weird people laying on their bellies, screaming their sins out. Or they cringe, because it sounds like something that will cut them off from all the fun and pleasure in their lives. But like many principles in God's kingdom, the very opposite is true. **It is by repentance that we gain our freedom.**

- How do you feel about God right now? Is He your best friend, or just an acquaintance? Or is He someone you stay as far away from as possible?
- Do you have past experiences where you felt God was nowhere to be found?
- Is there a chance you could still be angry with Him for 'letting you down' in your past?
- Are there areas in your life that you have had trouble letting God take control?

Oh boy!

Repentance is also critical because the Bible says that we will **perish** if we do not repent (Luke 13:3). It is human nature to put off until tomorrow what we should be doing today. Many of us think "Oh, I don't have time for God right now. I'm going to live the way I want until I'm done 'having fun', and then, at the last minute, I'll accept God in my life so I don't have to go to hell". But the Bible warns explicitly about this dangerous mindset. We may not have time to tell God we're sorry before our life is taken.

Scripture also warns us that unless our hearts are genuinely humble and repentant towards the Lord, our hearts can become so hardened that even if we see a person raised from the dead, we will still resist the truth that hell is awaiting us if we don't accept Christ! We *must* experience a 'softening' of our hearts, one that is truly sorry for our sin (Luke 16:19-31). God is just waiting to hear our remorseful confession, so He can help us out of our brokenness, and into a fulfilling, satisfying, and eternal relationship with Him.

What exactly does this relationship entail?

The Bible wisely tells us to 'count the cost' before we invest in anything, and that includes leaving our old life and embracing the life that Jesus offers (Luke 14:26-33). Following Jesus has phenomenal benefits, but it certainly is not a walk in the park! To begin with, we need to face our fears about letting go of what we are familiar with, because often, this is the very thing that keeps us from accepting the Lord. Some valid questions that people might ask before they commit their lives to Jesus include:

"Do I have to give up everything in my life that I consider 'fun'?"
"Do I have to bury my lifelong dreams?"
"Does this mean I can no longer be 'myself'?"
"Will I have to divorce my non-Christian spouse?"
"Do I have to give up my job?"

These are great questions and should definitely be answered to our satisfaction before we commit ourselves fully to God. We find that a big part of our question is answered in 1 Corinthians 7:17-24. This scripture wisely tells us to 'continue as we were before we accepted Christ'. And in verses 12-16, we see that we should stay married to an unbelieving spouse unless *they* choose to leave *us*.

This will undoubtedly be difficult, but you'll need to pray like crazy and behave in ways that please the Lord in order to win them to Christ! Jesus can be your new 'spouse' until there is peace among you. So, the bottom line is, unless we are living immorally, we should pretty much stay committed to what we were doing before we came to the Lord. He will work out the details.

"Christian" = 'misery'

Many non-Christians think that submitting their lives to God will just lead to misery. Ironically, they often say they understand God, the Bible, and the Christian life. And they have a multitude of excuses of why they can't or won't follow God's leading. But the scriptures tell us that people who are not indwelt by the Holy Spirit cannot really understand spiritual things (1 Corinthians 2:10-16). Therefore, people who don't believe in God and have not submitted their lives to Him may *say* they have read the Bible, but unless they have the Spirit of God living in them, they are literally *unable* to comprehend its truths.

God actually blinds their minds until they receive salvation! And He does this purposefully, so that those who 'think' they are wise will be confounded by their pride. However, the sinner who knows they need a Savior and accepts Him gladly will be given the ability to understand the simple message of the gospel (1 Corinthians 1:20-29).

Consequently, many unbelievers are deceived into thinking that living a Christian life will strip them of all pleasure. They think the Bible is just a bunch of rules and regulations. They just wait for Christians to make mistakes, so they can justify why they don't follow God. And sadly, even our culture encourages us to drop all restraints, reject God, and 'Do whatever that seems right to you'.

But scripture says that the result of this attitude is absolute stupidity (Psalm 14:1)! Not only that, but it says that when we resist God in our lives, we are considered evil and corrupt! The truth is, if we continue to reject Him and live life by our own rules, we are headed for spiritual death now, which will translate into eternal punishment at the end of our lives (Proverbs 14:12).

We have to realize that we are only given two options in this life. We can accept Jesus now and live in eternal glory, or we will reject Him here and go to hell for eternity (Matthew 13:37-43 and Matthew 22:1-14). Contrary to some popular ideas, we will not have a chance to make this decision after we die (Luke 12:8-9 and Luke 13:24-30). People who refuse to acknowledge and follow Christ typically try to ignore these scriptures, but denying the Truth doesn't make it any less true. And rejecting the saving power of Jesus *will* lead to eternal punishment (1 Corinthians 1:18 and Galatians 6:7-10).

But I need to 'find' myself!

We may also be deceived into thinking that we will lose our identity and our independence if we give our lives to God. But the truth is, we are not really 'ourselves' until we live in the ways that God has designed us. Sin distorts our original character, and who we 'become' outside of Christ is not who He intended for us to be. God created us, and He is the One Who put our desires, strengths, and talents into our minds, hearts, and spirits. Therefore, unless we are living alongside of Him, we will never develop into all that we were meant to be. There is a vitality and satisfaction that we were made to experience only while being IN relationship with Jesus!

Of course it's true that living for Christ *does* require self-control and obedience. We could probably all use a dose of these qualities, anyways! But when God is at the helm, we receive power from the Holy Spirit that is necessary to live a godly life. He is there *just to help us* please and glorify God! I certainly want to have the Lord's power and wisdom behind me when I'm making life's tough decisions; rather than being alone, and trying to muster up that strength and insight all by myself.

We face another problem when we choose to sin. We actually cover up our authentic selves. We use ungodly thoughts and behaviors to define our personality, and the person that God created is sadly hidden. Only the Lord has the power to set us free from our selfishness and self-centeredness. And only then will we have the liberty to become who we were really created to be.

Me, myself, and I

Do you ever feel like you're just fighting a 'headwind' in life? Like you just can't 'get ahead' mentally or emotionally? There are times when we don't even know why we are unhappy or dissatisfied. The truth is, we probably don't even realize that the reason we lack **real** joy and peace is because we are disconnected from the only One who can impart authentic joy and peace into our lives. When we live apart from a connection with God, Jesus, and the Holy Spirit, we are **incapable** of experiencing the deeply satisfying gifts that He has for us.

You might even be thinking that you could care less if you are far from God at this point in your life. You may believe that your life is running very smoothly without Him. You might even think that you live an 'upright' life. But all humans are guilty of being imperfect in one way or another, just by being alive! We *all* fall short of God's standards and we are all considered sinners in God's sight (Romans 3:21-28). Without the blood sacrifice of Jesus covering us and cleansing us, we are doomed.

Besides, if we are honest, we'll admit that most of us are either partially or fully controlled in one area or another by our ungodly passions. And the Bible says that you are literally a slave to whatever controls you (2 Peter 2:19), no matter how 'free' you might feel. Also remember that even though you may not be doing anything you *think* is wrong, our base sin as human beings is when we choose to reject Jesus, the Savior (John 16:9).

But when we place our lives in God's hands, He can finally use the qualities that *He* placed in us for the purposes that *He* intended. Just as a machine operates best when used according to the manufacturers' instructions, our lives function the most effectively and smoothly when they are handled by the Master. And the wonderful byproduct of this relationship will bring us peace with ourselves, others, and God, just the way He planned.

- List some differences between the person you are at home and the person you portray to those outside of your home.

What happens if we don't confess and repent?

Shame and guilt are emotions that seem to bring only embarrassment and pain. So we tend to avoid it, like many uncomfortable feelings. But we were **created** to feel guilty when we have done wrong. And healthy guilt can cause us to genuinely repent and to experience lasting change.

The problem is, if we only *say* we are sorry because we're trying to please others or because we've been 'caught', this will eventually lead to spiritual death (2 Corinthians 7:10). This is 'unhealthy guilt', and it keeps us from intimacy with Jesus, the Lover of our souls!

Because we often hide our sin from others, we usually keep the ugliness of our misdeeds bottled up inside of us (John 3:18-21). And in our shame, we tend to distance ourselves from God, others, and even ourselves. This leads to further misery and isolation. We then try to cover up our sin with false behavior, such as pretending that nothing is wrong. Maybe we indulge in our addictions, because this issue is too uncomfortable to deal with and we just want to forget what's going on. Interestingly, studies have proven that many physical and psychiatric illnesses are directly related to guilt, shame, and unforgiveness.

Let's use an example. Say you have done something wrong that you knew would hurt someone that you cared about, so you hide what you've done from them. Eventually, the guilt that you feel about your sin keeps you from having a close relationship with them, because your wrongdoing keeps popping up in your head whenever you're with them. And you feel like a fraud if you're nice to them, because you know you haven't been a loyal friend.

But if you decide to confess your mistake with heartfelt sorrow and they forgive you, the air is cleared, and you can once again enjoy an intimate bond. This is exactly how it is with God. Confession and repentance are essential if we want to enjoy the benefits of a close and authentic life with Christ (Psalm 51). This attitude of humility also keeps us from grieving the wonderful Holy Spirit (Ephesians 4:30).

It's also important to mention that our guilt (or lack of guilt) is not always a reliable indicator of a healthy relationship with the Lord or others. Unhealthy guilt can keep us enslaved, because we tend to isolate from others. On the other hand, our lack of guilt can also leave us distanced from others, because we are constantly trying to justify and shield our position.

Humans naturally have a tendency to gloss over their shortcomings, and denying our sin is common (Psalm 119:29). But over time, our repeated and unconfessed sin can make us insensitive, so that eventually, we don't even feel bad about what we have done. This is exactly what has happened to those who have committed violent crimes. While there are true psychopaths – people that truly have *no* conscience, they are rare. However, for most people who are extremely violent or perverse, their consciences have been hardened and burned over time, and they are incapable of feeling sorrow or pain anymore.

Lastly, there are times that we may not even feel sorry for what we have done. We fail to ask for forgiveness, because we think we have to 'feel' something in order to apologize. But this is a great time to ask God to change our hearts so that we DO feel sorry for the actions we take that are contrary to His ways.

<u>Beware – but don't get paranoid!</u>

Now before you get overly obsessed about every little sin you commit, it's important to realize that we will make many mistakes in our walk with Christ. There is a process of maturing in the Lord, and we will definitely fall once in a while! But we are in danger if we <u>continue</u> to rebel and refuse to live God's way (Hebrews 6:4-6).

The truth is, if we are really following Jesus, we should begin to display an increasing likeness to Him. The Bible says that God is not really in us, and we are *liars*, if we are Christians, but we purposefully continue to sin (1 John 2:3-6 and 1 John 3:7-10). Our sins should be more like a blip in the screen, as opposed to a regular practice.

It is our daily choices that make the difference between holiness and wickedness. Remember, in *every* decision we make, we are either choosing God's standards, or our own will (Matthew 12:30). The Bible says that there are *only* two camps – God's, and the devils'. There IS no middle ground (John 8:42-47). We need to beware - if we are choosing to live a *lifestyle* of sin after we accept Christ, we can get into some serious trouble (Hebrews 10:26-29).

Additionally, we may not be living in 'obvious' sin – you know, like murdering, lying, cheating, stealing, or sleeping around. But there are also insidious, or 'hidden' sins that can really destroy us, too. They come in the form of pride, rebellion, selfishness, and critical attitudes. These are our natural tendencies – the ones that God wants to change in us.

Satan is always there too, taunting and deceiving us. By the way, "The devil made me do it" is not written anywhere in the Bible! It is our own sinful flesh that makes us unholy (James 1:12-15). But Satan IS real, and he tries to use our own weaknesses to try to get us to do things **his** way or **our way,** instead of God's way.

Finally, there may be times when we confess and repent of our sin, but our guilt continues to eat us alive over our past mistakes. We can't seem to get the thoughts of what we have done out of our minds. This is the time when we need to immerse ourselves in the scriptures, because the Word of God is the means by which our hearts and minds are transformed.

Reading the Bible and obeying it trains our minds to believe the *truth* about our sin and God's forgiveness. It's essential that we learn to take hold of our thoughts and emotions and submit them to Jesus (2 Corinthians 10:3-5). While we need to accept that our sin brings death (Romans 6:23), just as importantly, we need to *know* that once we are forgiven, *we are forgiven* (1 John 1:9)!

- List some ways that you may not be honoring the Lord. Include the obvious sins, as well as some of the less noticeable attitudes you have (pride, selfishness, etc).

<u>How do I go about repenting?</u>

How do we pinpoint our sin? How can we overcome the attitudes and behaviors that are strangling us in our lives? We all know it's easy to see the glaring sins we commit. But many times, we don't really want to look inside to figure out *why* we continue making poor choices.

Many times, we have the willingness to follow God, but we have trouble knowing *how* to turn our lives around. John 15:1-14 gives us a model to follow that will help us change our thoughts and attitudes so that we *can* begin choosing God's ways.

The word often used in this chapter is 'remaining', or ABIDING in Christ. To 'abide' means to adhere, cleave, cling, stick, dwell, live, and/or reside, accept, and consent. The opposite of abiding is to leave, quit, move, evade, remove, shift, or depart.

Humility is required in order for us to repent. We need to admit that God is the only perfect Being, and that we cannot run our lives in the fullness that He has intended for us without His help. We find that the opposite of repentance is **disobedience**. If we are honest with ourselves, we will admit that when we live in sin, we do not display humility. Nor do we welcome change.

- Think about the words above and compare them to your relationship with God. Are you in a place where you are abiding in Him, or moving away from Him?

We can see from this scripture that following Jesus is a matter of 'accepting' His sacrifice. We 'consent' to His control and power in our lives. We 'adhere', or obey His standards as laid out in the Bible. We 'stick' to His principles when we are weak or feel like sinning. We 'cling' to Him for comfort and strength. And we allow Him to 'dwell', or live, in our hearts and minds. THIS is the essence of Christian living. Remember, Jesus knows we cannot overcome our old lives by ourselves. That is exactly why He chose to die in our place, and why He chose to have the Holy Spirit to live inside of us (Romans 8:1-14).

As we consistently choose to abide in Christ Jesus, He promises to change the desires of our hearts so we will *want* to live a holy life (Psalm 37:3-4). It takes time to change and grow, so if you aren't completely different in a week, don't think that Jesus isn't helping you. Just as a seed that is put in the ground takes time to bring us beautiful fruit and flowers, we need to be grounded in His love and His Word over time in order to reap a beautiful and lasting harvest.

Jesus also promises to guide our steps if we seek His will in ALL we do (Proverbs 3:5-6). And He promises to take care of our needs *if* we put His kingdom **first** in our lives (Matthew 6:33). We exchange our mess for His perfection! He wants to have an intimate relationship with us, and He died to prove it (John 3:16-17 and Romans 5:8).

How do we know if we are living the way God wants us to?

If we think we have 'repented' , but our behavior has not changed, then we need to reexamine our motives. Why have we repented? If we are 'repenting' just to feel better, or because we 'should', or to please someone, or just to get out of trouble, then we will not experience any change in our hearts or actions. And we won't receive the blessings of a cleansed conscience, because our motives are impure. Remember, God is

Truth, and if we aren't coming to Him *truthfully*, then we will fail to reap the benefits of a genuine relationship with Him.

This is exactly the situation where we meet people who conclude that they have 'tried' Christianity, but they've decided it doesn't 'work' for them. Actually, Jesus is not at all the problem – the reality is that *they* haven't really turned from their old lives, nor have they completely given their hearts and their minds over to the Lord.

Maybe you are 'repenting' just because you want to make others think you are a good person. In reality, the only reason to repent is *because we love the Lord and don't want to hurt Him.* If we really care for Him, we will want to change our hearts and minds. And God will give us the power by His Holy Spirit.

Additionally, if others know that we are Christians but our lives are polluted, then we will destroy our witness for Jesus. Make no mistake – people WATCH Christians to see how they act. And we often give them a reason to pile on the excuses as to why they don't want anything to do with God or the church, because they see us living a hypocritical life.

The only way to tell if our repentance is genuine is by our resultant behavior (Luke 3:8-9). We should be able to see growth in our lives if we are truly moving closer to Jesus. It is only by repentance that we can be baptized. We then receive forgiveness, and the gift of the Holy Spirit (Acts 2:38). And the most important part is that we need to repent in order to receive the gift of eternal life (Acts 11:18).

Is your repentance genuine?

We need to continually examine ourselves in the light of God's Word. If you 'say' you love God, but are still:

using your old ways of thinking,

treating people in your old, harsh, selfish manner,

full of bitterness,
full of unforgiveness,
continuing in your addictions,
using profanity or pornography,
frequently in a rage,
or engaged in <u>any</u> sexual sin,

then you have not truly repented. Furthermore, if you are one of God's children and you *continue* to refuse to change, then you are living in **rebellion.** And there is no good thing that comes from this attitude (1 Samuel 15:22-23a). It's interesting that it mentions that rebellion is as bad as witchcraft, because witchcraft is absolutely prohibited by God (Deuteronomy 18:9-14). He even says that anyone who does these things is *detestable* to Him (verse12). And it also says in this scripture that stubbornness is as bad as idol worship. God strictly forbids worshiping idols, as well, and its seriousness is displayed in the fact that it is listed in the very first two of the Ten Commandments.

On the other hand, if we are genuinely repenting, we will see positive fruit, such as:

a new compassion for others,
a heart for the lost,
grief over sin (Psalm 51),
revulsion for our ungodly lifestyles,
feeling increasingly uncomfortable when we sin
power to overcome our negative attitudes
and experiencing a new, deep joy as a result of living a holy life (Psalm 32).

Again, we don't get here overnight. But make sure that you *are* changing somewhat over time.

- Compare your attitudes to the ones listed above. How are they similar? Different?

Real Change!

After we have confessed our sins to God, it is time to begin allowing the Holy Spirit to change our minds, hearts, and feelings, so that our behavior changes. If we admit our sin and then do nothing about it, we have missed the entire reason for confession. The great news is, that unlike the world, we have the POWER to change! People that do not have God in their lives try to change by moving to new locations, modifying their habits and behaviors, reading self-help books, attending unhealthy support groups, hanging out with new people, or finding new jobs to get away from their old situations. But their problems follow them because they are unable to change their TRUE desires. Only the Spirit of God can do that!

That is not to say that trying to improve ourselves is wrong. And we certainly *do* need the support of other healthy, growing Christians. But if we expect **anything** besides the power of the Living God to change our ungodly desires, then we are fooling ourselves and setting ourselves up for failure and disappointment (Deuteronomy 8:18; Colossians 1:11-14; 2 Peter 1:3-9).

But I don't need GOD to help me change!

This might bring up the subject of people you might have seen who seem to have 'changed' *without* God in their lives. You might wonder if having a relationship with God *is* really necessary in order to change. Maybe you have a friend who used to use drugs and just quit cold turkey. Possibly you know someone who used to sleep around and use terrible language, but now is settled down with a family, and doesn't act like that anymore.

The truth is that people who change without God may have changed behavior, but there is a difference between behavior modification and a deep, true, heart change. Sometimes we grow out of certain behaviors, and other times, we can force ourselves to change. These are mental and physical changes, sort of an 'action change'.

But behavior that is changed without the power of the Lord is usually either short-lived, or it is lived without much joy. *Remember, we can change our behavior, but we are unable to change our desires without God's intervention.*

However, when God gets involved, the desires of our hearts change so that we begin to want the things God wants for us. We experience a supernatural power that is much greater than ours. When we live by this motivation, it's much easier to live God's way. And we'll find that we won't be obeying because we *have* to.

I have heard many people say "I would have done anything to get that drug or that person before I met Jesus. But I don't want that in my life anymore". That is the miracle of God working in our lives. As we continue living by God's power and wisdom, we will find a new peace, because we are obeying the Lord's will with all of our hearts, minds, and strength – with delight!

Most importantly, if we reject God, we are shutting out the Person who created us. Much of our makeup as humans is spiritual, and we're really ignoring a big part of *ourselves* if we keep Jesus out of our lives. And if we decide to awaken our 'spiritual' side with anyone or anything but God the Father, God the Son, and God the Holy Spirit, we are inviting demonic activity into our lives. You may gasp and say "I am not dealing with Satan!" But the truth is, there are *only* two sides – that of the devil and that of Jesus Christ (John 8:42-47).

Also, be aware that there are several religious groups that call themselves Christians. However, they do not believe that **Jesus is God**. This is the entire foundation of our faith! You can discern a genuine Christian from a false follower by what they believe about this critical fact of Jesus' Deity (John 1;1-5, and verse 14; John 14:9-11; Ephesians 1:19-23; Philippians 2:5-11; Colossians 1:15-20; and Hebrews 1:2-3).

Jesus Himself says "**I** am the Way, the Truth, and the Life. No one comes to the Father but by **Me**" (John 14:6-7). This is essential to understand and believe, because *this* is what sets real Christ-followers apart from any other religion or false sect. And this is why Christ deserves our complete adoration and life devotion.

What are the benefits of repentance?

We've learned that after we choose to turn away from our sin, we need to turn TO Jesus. Stagnation is not a godly attribute! When we repent, it cleanses us so that we can have a clean conscience, which helps to purify our faith (1Timothy 1:5). God wants to foster new attitudes in us; confessing and repenting of our sins actually benefits *us*. You have probably heard the old saying "You are only as sick as your secrets". And that is absolutely true in our Christian walk.

We also need confession and repentance so that we can worship the Lord (Hosea 14:2 and Nehemiah 9:2-3). When our faith is pure, we can worship in Spirit and in Truth, which is what He desires (John 4:23-24).

God says that He literally *wipes our sins away* when we genuinely repent. When we turn from our sin, our relationship with Him is restored, so that we can share in His presence once again. Our world is looking for refreshment of their souls. A relationship that is untainted by sin with our Savior is exactly the place we experience this rejuvenation (Acts 3:19-20).

And don't forget that heaven *rejoices* when a sinner gives their life to Christ (Luke 15:8-10). Just imagine the sight – angels everywhere singing and laughing because ONE person turned their will, desires, motives, dreams, fears, hearts, and minds over to the will of God.

- Have you had the pleasure of having your sins forgiven and experiencing the freedom and joy associated with it? Write down one example.

Tools of the trade

Reading and *obeying* the Bible is one of the most effective resources we need for the direction, power, and motivation to overcome our sin (James 4:17). The Word of God is supernatural, and it allows us a deep understanding of ourselves that we just can't find in 'self-help' books or other people. It gives us insight so that we can recognize our motives – that is, what is really in our hearts and minds. And far from the belief that we are all basically 'nice' people, Jeremiah 17:9 says that the human heart is **deceitfully wicked**.

Many times, even *we* can't even figure out what it is that makes us act the way we do! But the Bible is ALIVE and powerful and is able to explain our condition very nicely ☺ (Hebrews 4:12). The written Word of God exposes us for who we really are. It points out what is wrong in our lives, teaches us what is right, and gives us power to change through the Spirit of God (2 Timothy 3:16).

And of course, prayer is another vital tool that we must use constantly to stay in touch with our 'Power Source', the Lord. We read in 1 Thessalonians 5:17 that we are never to stop praying. This doesn't mean that we stay on our knees twenty four hours a day. Rather, it means that we stay mindful of the Lord constantly throughout our day. Whenever we have questions, worries, or fears, we pray for wisdom, direction, and comfort. When we feel wonderful and confident, we pray, giving our thanks to God. And when we feel weak, lost, or confused, we ask Him for power, stability, and assurance. We truly *can* pray all day long.

The last tool that is critical in our arsenal of spiritual weapons is our choice to spend time with those that live genuinely godly lives. Even if someone 'calls' themselves a Christian, but gossips, lies, frequently complains, or is involved in sexual sin, that person is just as bad of an influence as a nonbeliever.

Also, when we long for our old life and the people associated with it, the Bible says that we are not fit for the kingdom of God (Luke 9:62)! If we try to keep one foot in our past and one foot in the kingdom, we will *absolutely* fail in our walk with the Lord (James 1:5-8).

If we use these three basic tools – the Bible, prayer, and fellowship with strong Christians – then we will be able to cultivate a deep, intimate, and lasting relationship with the Lord. And in doing this, we will find our sin much easier to overcome.

- Are you using any of the tools listed here? Are you willing to start disciplining yourself in order to use them?

<u>Don't be deceived</u>

It bears repeating - even some people who call themselves Christians may not be living a godly life. If your 'Christian' friends are living immorally in any way, then get away from them (Proverbs 1:10 and 4:14-15). And take heed yourself - Jesus says that a half-hearted Christian is worse than one who coldly rejects Him altogether (Revelation 3:15-16). The Greek word for 'spit' in this scripture is literally **vomit.** That scares me.

God cannot use people who 'call' themselves by His holy Name, but they live just like everyone else. They lack the power to stand for righteousness. These people have not truly repented (turned from their sin and genuinely turned to God's ways). And worse, they turn nonbelievers away from the faith (Matthew 18:2-6).

The Bible says that a tree is judged by its fruit (Matthew 7:15-20). The verses that follow have a stern warning for us (Matthew 7:21-23). If others can't see our faith by our actions, then our faith is dead (James 2:14-25). God calls us into *active* obedience, and if we do what He asks, He promises to give us the desire and the power to do His will (Philippians 2:13). But it is *our* choice. Obedience and holiness begins with our own choices.

So the bottom line is, if we choose to stay in *close* relationships with those who are not exhibiting love, joy, peace, patience, kindness, goodness, faithfulness, gentleness, and self control (Galatians 5:22-23), we will be much more likely to drift into a powerless Christian life. And we will most likely be drawn away from our faith altogether, before we persuade them to live a life of righteousness for Christ (2 Peter 3:17-18 and Revelation 2:4-5). While we do need to spend time with unbelievers to influence them for God, the people we spend the most time with should definitely be those who live authentic Christian lives.

The secret to fulfillment

God created us with a place in our souls that can only be filled by Him. That's why we feel so empty even after we have exhausted all our energy trying to obtain peace and joy. We have a tendency in our culture to constantly run around doing things, but we have a very difficult time sitting still and being quiet. The Bible tells us how to live a life of purpose and hope, but it requires spending private time with God. We need the solitude and quiet so that we can read the Bible and hear God speaking to us.

If we discipline ourselves in this manner, our minds will soon begin to understand the things of God. We will become aware of His leading throughout our days. If we are obedient to what we have learned during this quiet time, we will be filled with a sense of satisfaction and peace that we have never known before. Remember, this kind of obedience is NOT religious, robot-like behavior. When we abide in Jesus, He becomes our trusted friend and reliable teacher. When we fall in love with Him, we soon *desire* His will above ours.

We have to assess our own lives. Are we turning away from Christ's mighty power to save us by disobeying Him again and again? Is God calling you to change something in your life, and you are stubbornly refusing to amend your ways? Please realize that your heart IS getting harder and harder EVERY time you deny His truth. The real danger is that you will end up turning away from God completely. And this will cause you to blame Him, instead of admitting that it was your own stubbornness and pride that kept you from submitting to His authority in the first place.

We are not perfect! But we should be increasingly laying down our sin as it is revealed to us. We should begin to despise whatever it is in us that is NOT like Jesus. We should begin experiencing more self-love, because we were created in His image. Our old behavior should be in the *daily* process of moving out! This happens as our minds are transformed by the Word of God (Romans 12:2), prayer, and hanging out with Christians who actually 'walk the talk'. And in time, we should be growing in the Lord, not continuing to take 'baby steps' forever (1 Corinthians 3:1-3 and Hebrews 6:1). Your way does not work! It will never work!

My prayer and deep desire for you is to truly admit it all to God. Tell Him that you're weak. Share your struggles and sins with Him. Ask Him for a soft heart, one that wants to obey. He will never turn this godly attitude away (Psalm 51:17). You can pray for the desire to change and live God's way. It is never too late, and there is nothing you have done that is so terrible that it cannot be forgiven. Eternity may not look like a big deal now, but you don't want to find out you made the wrong choice when you stand in front of God on that day. Help us Lord, to turn *from* our sin and *to* You.

Today is the day of repentance!

REFLECTION

1. What is repentance?

2. How do you know if someone is truly repentant?

3. What are some of your idols (things in your life you put above your interest in God or His kingdom)? This can include food, television, your kids or spouse, money, work, ungodly reading material, clothes, computer, etc). "Idols" are defined by what you spend your time, energy and/or money on.

4. What happens if we do not repent?

5. What is keeping you from true repentance?

   Fear?

   Pride?

   Stubborness?

   Laziness?

   Unforgiveness?

6. What do you plan to do to get closer to God? (James 4:8).

NOTES

REFLECTION WORKSHEET

Following is a worksheet to help you define the areas in which you need to repent. It should be filled out slowly, thoughtfully, and prayerfully. You only need to write something by the sentences that apply to you. You can also write down what comes to mind when you read each sentence, even if it doesn't *completely* relate to your situation. And even if something *seems* like it doesn't apply to you, ask God to reveal hidden agendas and motives in your heart. Then, ask Him to help you face and overcome these issues in your life.

Lord, I repent of: (This can be any obvious sins, like drinking, sleeping around, lying or cheating)

____

I repent of: (the less obvious sins – pride, selfishness, blaming others for all my troubles, gossip, slander, hoarding my things or money, etc).

I don't know how to repent.

I don't know what repentance is.

I don't know what it is that I need to repent of. Please show me.

Help me to WANT to see my sin clearly.

I need to repent of my unforgiveness. I WANT to let go of the feelings I hold onto against those who have hurt me. It helps if you begin by naming people who quickly come to your mind, and then, pray about those in your past that you have been reluctant to think about because it's too painful.

I need to repent of judging others.

I need to repent of wasting time.

I need to repent of spending time only on myself.

I need to repent of worry, anxiety, and/or lack of trust in You.

I want to repent of my stubbornness (wanting to do it my way all the time).

I want to repent of a hard heart.

I need to repent of my pride (thinking my way is always better than Yours, or others)

I need to repent of my fear (I am afraid of letting go)

I am afraid of the future

I am afraid of God

I am afraid of myself

Lord, I don't know You very well, and I don't feel I can trust You completely yet

I don't understand Your ways and I fear them

I need to repent of my disobedience

I need to repent of my refusal to change

I need to repent of my selfishness

I need to repent of hating myself

I need to repent of my old life

The drugs or alcohol I took to hurt my body

The people I hurt in the process of living my old life

I need to repent of my complaining

I need to repent of my lack of worship for God

I need to repent of my critical spirit

I need to repent of my lack of love for others (this love is genuinely putting other's needs above yours. This does not just encompass your family, or those that are easy to love. This area includes people that are *unlovely* in your life. It especially means those you have to go out of your comfort zone to help).

I need to repent of my lack of affection for people

Lord,
I know in my heart that I am not living close to You. I want to pray now for help so that I can change. I want to experience the love, joy, peace, hope, and purpose that You have for me. I have been living life by my rules and my desires for so long, I am afraid to approach You with my sin and waywardness. And I'm afraid to give up control of my life. Please change my heart so that I *want* to be right with You.
And please give me the courage to be honest with You. Your Word says that You will not turn away a person who is truly asking for help. It also says that You DIED for my sin because I couldn't pay the price. I come before You now and ask for the desire and the power to get close to You, and to begin to live the way that You want me to live.
In Jesus name, Amen.

Made in the USA
San Bernardino, CA
21 July 2018